101 Questions and Answers on Deacons

101 QUESTIONS AND ANSWERS ON DEACONS

William T. Ditewig

Paulist Press
New York/Mahwah, N.J.

Nihil Obstat:
Rev. Isidore Dixon
Censor Deputatus

Imprimatur:
Reverend Monsignor Godfrey Mosley
Vicar General for the Archdiocese of Washington

February 11, 2004

Scripture extracts are taken from the New Revised Standard Version, Copyright © 1993 and 1989, by the Division of Christian Education of the National Council of the Churches of Christ in the United States of America and reprinted by permission of the publisher. All rights reserved.

Extracts from the Documents of the Second Vatican Council are the Author's translation and from Walter Abbot's edition of *The Documents of Vatican II* © 1966 by America Press used by kind permission of America Press. Visit: www.americamagazine.org.

The cover design of the Trini Cross with the traditional Deacon's stole is courtesy of Deacon Bill Scarmardo for Pax Creations, Inc. www.paxcreations.com, 866-PAX-6373.

Book design by Theresa M. Sparacio

Cover design by Cynthia Dunne

Library of Congress Cataloging-in-Publication Data

Ditewig, William T.
    101 questions and answers on deacons / William T. Ditewig.
      p. cm.
    Includes bibliographical references.
    ISBN 0-8091-4265-1 (alk. paper)
    1. Deacons. I. Title: One hundred one questions and answers on deacons. II. Title: One hundred and one questions and answers on deacons. III. Title.
BV680.D56 2004
262′.142—dc22

2004008866

Published by Paulist Press
997 Macarthur Boulevard
Mahwah, New Jersey 07430

www.paulistpress.com

Printed and bound in the
United States of America

CONTENTS

FOR MY FAMILY,
WITH LOVE AND THANKS

AND FOR ALL WHO SERVE

If then there is any encouragement in Christ, any consolation from love, any sharing in the Spirit, any compassion and sympathy, make my joy complete: be of the same mind, having the same love, being in full accord and of one mind. Do nothing from selfish ambition or conceit, but in humility regard others as better than yourselves. Let each of you look not to your own interests, but to the interests of others. Let the same mind be in you that was in Christ Jesus,

who, though he was in the form of God,
    did not regard equality with God
    as something to be exploited,
but emptied himself,
    taking the form of a slave,
    being born in human likeness.
And being found in human form,
    he humbled himself
    and became obedient to the point of death—
    even death on a cross.

Therefore God also highly exalted him
    and gave him the name
    that is above every name,
so that at the name of Jesus
    every knee should bend,
    in heaven and on earth and under the earth,
and every tongue should confess
    that Jesus Christ is Lord,
    to the glory of God the Father.

Philippians 2:1–11

INTRODUCTION: DEACONS IN THE CONTEMPORARY CHURCH

> The service of the deacon is the Church's service sacramentalized.
>
> John Paul II, *Address to Permanent Deacons*

When I was growing up in central Illinois in the 1950s and early 1960s, ministry in the Catholic Church seemed a relatively straightforward matter. At St. Patrick Church on the South Side of Peoria, Illinois, Monsignor Patrick O'Connor Culleton reigned as pastor. Born in 1877 in County Kilkenny, he was educated and ordained in Ireland. However, shortly after ordination as a priest in 1900, he came to the Diocese of Peoria, where he served the rest of his long life. After serving in various parishes, he was appointed pastor of St. Patrick's in 1923, and he remained there until his death in 1960. (He became the first mentor of a young, newly ordained priest named Fulton J. Sheen, who served in his first parish assignment at St. Patrick's under Monsignor's tute- lage. Archbishop Sheen would later recall that Monsignor Culleton was the holiest priest he ever knew.) When he died in 1960, Monsignor presided over a staff that included three priests and a large contingent of the School Sisters of Notre Dame, who had long staffed the St. Patrick Grade School. There was one lay woman who taught at St. Patrick School (the wonderful Mrs.

Brophy, who taught third grade), but I think most of us saw her as a teacher, not as a minister. Official *ministry* was something that was done by Monsignor, the other priests, and the sisters. In fact, to be perfectly frank, "ministry" was a word more associated with Protestant ministers than with Catholic clergy and religious.

This limited vision of ministry was expanded a bit in the early 1960s when a new Catholic high school was built in Peoria. Bergan High School was unique for many reasons, but in terms of ministry, it was significant because it was staffed by Christian Brothers. For many of us, this was the first time we had met men in ministry who were not priests.

In short, if you were a boy and interested in ministry, you could become a priest or a brother; if you were a girl, you could become a religious sister. I don't think that many in our generation realized just how quickly and dramatically this perception of ministry would change when the Second Vatican Council opened on October 11, 1962. When I entered high school seminary in September 1963, there were more than 125 members of our freshman class alone, and all of us had the intention of becoming priests. In fact, there were so many high school seminaries in the state of Wisconsin at that time that we needed two basketball divisions (East and West) to accommodate all of them! All of this was about to change, suddenly, and with the force of a hurricane.

Blessed Pope John XXIII took most of the world by surprise when, less than one hundred days after his election in October 1958, and two months following his seventy-seventh birthday, he announced his intention to convoke the twenty-first General Council of the Church. The day of this announcement, January 25, 1959, marked the beginning of a remarkable period of excitement and creativity in the Church. The central task of the Council was to address the relationship of the Church to the contemporary world, a world that had experienced so much tragedy, bloodshed, and violence in the twentieth century. Pope John wanted to throw open the windows of the Church to see if the Gospel could be proclaimed more effectively in these modern times. To do this, he called upon the bishops of the world to gather together in solemn assembly at the Vatican. As pastors, they could debate, discuss, and deliberate the pastoral activities the Church should undertake. Since this would be the second time the bishops had gathered at the Vatican, the Council became known as the Second Vatican Council, or simply, Vatican II.

To say that the Second Vatican Council was an extraordinary event does not do it justice. More than 2600 bishops from around the world gathered. This was more than three times the number that had attended the previous Council, Vatican I, in 1869–1870. But not only were the numbers themselves impressive; the presence of bishops from all over the world was most significant. For example, the third-largest national body of bishops to attend the Council were from Brazil! The points of view expressed by the bishops at the Council would truly reflect the worldwide experience of church in all of its great diversity.

The Council had many serious tasks ahead of it, none more significant perhaps than coming to grips with what it meant to be a worldwide "Church of Christ" in the modern world. What is this Church, how does one become a member of it, how is it structured, and what is its mission in the world? How do the members of the Church relate to each other and to the world in which they live and work? In working out answers to some of these questions, the bishops chose to describe the Church herself as a pilgrim people of God, the mystical Body of Christ, and the temple of the Holy Spirit. All persons, regardless of their state of life, are called to perfection in holiness, and to bear the "cost of discipleship" by living out in their lives the mission and ministry of Christ. The bishops spent considerable time addressing the nature and role of apostolic ministry in the Church, a ministry exercised in its fullness by bishops. This ministry is then shared by the bishop with other ministers in the Church, both those who are ordained and those who are not ordained. The source of ministry in the Church is Christ, and the right, power, and obligation to minister comes from the sacramental initiation of baptism. Some among the baptized receive a further consecration through sacramental ordination to serve the ministry of the rest.

In other words, in contrast to the experience most of us shared prior to the Council, the bishops described ministry as something to which *all* the baptized are called, not just those who are ordained or in religious communities. The role of the laity in ministry to the Church but most especially in the world was proclaimed strongly. The Council taught that through baptism and confirmation, all Catholics have an obligation to spread the good news through word and deed. The Council's teaching had forever changed the landscape of *ministry*.

The Council also recast our understanding of the nature of ordained ministry. The Council developed the Church's understanding of herself and her relationship to the world in which she lives. Within this expanded self-understanding came a renewed vision of ordained ministry as a service to the Church and to the world. The Council described ordained ministry as a participation in the ministry of the apostles. This apostolic ministry is received in its fullness through sacramental ordination as a bishop, and the bishop further shares this ministry when he ordains others into ministry. This is demonstrated graphically in the composition of chapter three of the *Dogmatic Constitution on the Church*. This chapter consists of twelve sections, numbered 18 through 29. The first ten sections (#18–#27) discuss apostolic ministry and the nature and role of the bishop. Only after this is done do we come to one paragraph (#28) on priests, and another (#29) on deacons.

It seems pretty clear that if one is to understand the nature of ordained ministry in the Church, one must first understand the nature and role of the bishop. The Council describes the apostolic ministry of the bishop as a *diakonia,* which is a Greek word meaning "service" (and is also the root word for "deacon"). This *diakonia* is threefold: a ministry of Word, of sacrament, and of charity. Priests and deacons, through their own sacramental ordination by a bishop, share in lesser ways in this threefold *diakonia*.

The ministerial landscape had been forever changed, but even today the implications of the Church's teaching through the Second Vatican Council continue to be worked out as new forms of ministry seek to coexist and collaborate with older forms, and as an older paradigm of ministry gives way to a newer one. Part of this new paradigm of ministry — and the focus of this book — is the ministry of deacons.

In one sense, the deacon had long been absent from the collective consciousness of the Church's ministry; in another, deacons had never actually been absent. Deacons had simply become part of a transitional passage of formation leading to eventual and ultimate ordination as priests. With the Second Vatican Council, deacons again walked from the wings of history onto the stage of permanent ordained ministry in their own right.

On June 18, 1967, with the promulgation of the document *Sacrum Diaconatus Ordinem* (the first three Latin words of the document, which mean "The Sacred Order of the Diaconate"), Pope Paul VI implemented the decision of the Second Vatican Council to revive the order of deacons as a permanent ministry in the Latin Rite of the Catholic Church.[1]

By 1970 there were some one hundred Latin Rite deacons serving around the world (only two of those deacons were in the United States). Today there are nearly 30,000 deacons, with almost 14,000 serving in the United States. The diaconate is thriving in many parts of the world, and yet for many people, the diaconate remains largely a mystery. This book hopes to address at least some of the more common questions that people have about deacons and the diaconate.

Many of these questions relate to the *functions* that deacons perform, and unfortunately, these are often the first questions that get asked. I say "unfortunately," because ordained ministry is always much more than simply a question of functions. We all know, for example, that "being a priest" is more than simply the performance of priestly functions; we know that "being a bishop" is more than celebrating the sacraments of confirmation and orders, sometimes referred to as "Holy (or Sacred) Orders." This is true of married life as well, and those who are married know full well that marriage as a sacrament is much more than simply an amalgam of the activities of married life: there is ineffable richness and depth to the bond between husbands and wives that transcends simple function. Even the language we use about these sacraments indicates that their essence lies beyond function: we speak of "*being* married," or "*being* a priest": the emphasis is on the "being," not on the doing.

So, what is "being a deacon" all about? What is the essence that lies behind the functions? Why was the diaconate revived by the Second Vatican Council? How did the bishops at the Council even know to bring the subject up? In order to dig into these questions, I have divided the book into two parts. The first four chapters deal generally with the *essence* of the diaconate: who deacons *are*. Only after that is done will we move to the next three chapters that deal with what deacons *do*.

Put simply, to understand deacons and their ministry, we must see the Church in a new way, through the eyes of the bishops of the Second Vatican Council. At the very end of the Council, Pope Paul VI reflected on the work of the Council and what it meant to the Church. In his homily of December 7, 1965, the day before the solemn closing of Vatican II, the Pope told his brother bishops:

> We stress that the teaching of the Council is channeled in one direction, the service of humankind, of every condition, in every weakness and need. The Church has declared herself a servant of humanity at the very time when her teaching role and her pastoral government have, by reason of this Church solemnity, assumed greater splendor and vigor. However, the idea of *service* has been central [emphasis added].[2]

This new vision of the Church-as-servant finds a concrete sacramental expression within the renewed diaconate; Pope Paul VI would later write that the diaconate is a "driving force for the Church's *diakonia* and a sacrament of the Lord Christ himself, who 'came not to be served but to serve.' "[3]

A recent article posed the question, "Are Deacons the Answer?"[4] Of course, the crucial response is to ask, "The answer to *what*?" If deacons are being proposed as a response to a shortage of priests, then they are *not* the answer. If deacons are being proposed out of a desire to emphasize clerical ministry over lay ministry, then they are *not* the answer. Rather, it is important to realize that the diaconate is not *the* answer to anything. It is, however, *part* of an answer. The question is, "How shall we best follow Christ in taking care of each other?" There are many ways of serving the Church and each other; we need *all* of them. The Church is a choir: the diaconate is simply one voice among the many. The balanced harmonies and inspiring melodies that emerge from a well-trained choir can transform the human heart.

ONE

DEACONS AND THE DIACONATE

The permanent diaconate…
a driving force for the Church's service.
Paul VI, *Ad pascendum*

1. Just who and what is a deacon anyway?

A Catholic deacon is a member of the clergy. In the Catholic Church, "the clergy" consists of three groups of ordained ministers: bishops, deacons, and priests. While all members of the Church are called to minister to others by virtue of their baptism, some Catholics are also ordained to specific forms of ministry to the rest of the Church. We refer to these ordained Catholics as "clerics" or "clergy."

The title "deacon" comes from the Greek word *diakonos*, which means "servant." A deacon is ordained by the bishop into the Order of Deacons (sometimes referred to simply as the "diaconate"), much like a priest is ordained into the Order of Presbyters (the "presbyterate"), and a bishop is ordained into the Order of Bishops (the "episcopate"). We will talk more about these three orders a bit later, and what ordination means. For now, however, it is enough to say that, once ordained a deacon by the bishop, the deacon enters into a new set of relationships: He is permanently and publicly configured to Christ the Servant, he shares in the overall pastoral responsibility of the bishop to care for all of the people in the diocese, and he becomes an integral part of the clerical structure of the Church, in partnership with priests, serving the needs of the entire diocese.

2. So are you saying that the deacon is a kind of priest?

No, not at all. Catholics are very familiar with the role of the priest in their communities, but for many people, deacons are still rather new. Since deacons are members of the clergy, they have responsibilities very similar to priests in some ways: They participate in a unique way in the Mass, they are official teachers and preachers of the Gospel, and they preside at celebrations of baptism, matrimony, funerals, and other forms of community prayer. They also share in the responsibility of outreach that one often associates with priests: Deacons visit the sick, the homebound, those imprisoned and in need. In this regard, there is certainly a "family resemblance" to the priesthood!

On the other hand, deacons have a unique expression of ordained ministry. The deacon is a particular "icon" or sacramental sign of Christ, who came "not to be served but to serve" (Mark 10:45). In this regard, the deacon has a profound responsibility to pour out his own life in service to others, just as Christ did. Therefore, while you will certainly see deacons participating in the Mass and other liturgical ceremonies, and for very good reasons, you may often *not* see the main thrust of the deacon's ministry, which is to be this sacramental sign of Christ outside the sanctuary, outside the church building and ecclesial structures. Deacons find themselves (or should, anyway!) in activities that others may not want or be able to tackle. As we will see later, deacons have a unique role in helping the Church link the two great commandments of Christ: "You shall love the Lord your God with all your heart, and with all your soul, and with all your mind. This is the greatest and first commandment. And a second is like it: 'You shall love your neighbor as yourself.' On these two commandments hang all the law and the prophets" (Matt 22:37–40).

3. Is being a deacon the same in all churches and denominations?

No. In some Protestant churches, a deacon is more like a parish trustee than an ordained minister. However, in other churches, such as Episcopalian and Methodist churches, the permanent diaconate is flourishing much as it is in the Catholic Church, and the duties of these deacons are very similar to ours. For example, they proclaim the Gospel and preach, they often lead the community prayer, and most significantly, they lead the community in outreach and the service of others.

The growing appreciation of the nature and role of the diaconate in a number of Protestant churches is taking place for a number of reasons. Some churches have observed the renewal of the diaconate in the Catholic Church and decided that this would be a positive development in their own church. More significant, however, is the fact that many of the same root conditions that caused the diaconate to be renewed by the Second Vatican Council (which we'll examine in some detail below) are not restricted to the Catholic experience.

4. When I was younger, we only talked about priests (and bishops) as clergy. Are deacons mentioned in the Bible?

Yes! The Hebrew Scriptures contain a number of references that relate to the responsibility of the people called by God to provide for those in need, although no one is specifically a minister of service in the same way that Christianity would develop the office. Deacons—as holders of some sort of ecclesial office—are first mentioned in the New Testament, although we don't know precisely what their duties were. We can get a hint from the first letter of Timothy (3:8–13), where we find the qualifications necessary for bishops and deacons. After discussing the requirements for bishops, the author continues:

> Deacons likewise must be serious, not double-tongued, not indulging in much wine, not greedy for money; they must hold fast to the mystery of the faith with a clear conscience. And let them first be tested; then, if they prove themselves blameless, let them serve as deacons. Women likewise must be serious, not slanderers, but temperate, faithful in all things. Let deacons be married only once, and let them manage their children and their households well; for those who serve well as deacons gain a good standing for themselves and great boldness in the faith that is in Christ Jesus.

From the very beginning, deacons have been close collaborators with the bishops of the Church. Deacons are frequently
mentioned in the writings of the fathers of the Church as ministers
who assist with the care of newcomers, of the poor, of widows and
orphans, and even in matters of justice. While the functions these
deacons fulfilled were varied and wide-ranging, there was always
a strong link between the deacon and the bishop, in whose name
the deacon served. One of the earliest references to deacons
teaches that deacons are ordained "not for priesthood but for service to the bishop."[5] In other places, deacons are described as the
"eyes" of the bishop, and even his "hearing, mouth, heart, and
soul"; the bishop and deacon are described as being as close as
father and son in the care of the people; in fact the bishop and deacon should be "like one soul dwelling in two bodies."[6]

Deacons were more than mere functionaries assisting the
bishop. St. Ignatius of Antioch, for example, described the role of
the bishop as similar to the role of God the Father, the role of
priests as similar to that of the apostles, and the role of deacons as
the ministry of Jesus the Christ, who poured out his own life to
reconcile and to save others.[7] The deacon is a sacramental witness
to Christ within the community, and the deacon also serves as a
prophetic reminder to all the baptized of their own responsibility
to care for others. Indeed, deacons are a sacramental sign of the
very diaconal nature of the Church herself.

5. If deacons are mentioned in scripture and in the writings of the early Church, why did they disappear for so long?

Actually, deacons were never really absent from the Church;
the Church has simply used deacons in different ways over the
centuries. As noted above, deacons have been a part of Church life
since her earliest days. What changed over time was that men
already ordained as deacons were later ordained as priests and, in
many cases, as bishops. In the early days of the Church, bishops
were elected by the priests (and sometimes by representatives of

the whole community); often the person best suited to succeed the bishop was his primary assistant, the deacon. The role of that early bishop was not unlike that of a modern priest-pastor of today: He was the on-the-scene leader of a specific community of believers.

As the Church continued to grow, and more communities developed, it became impossible for bishops to preside personally over each one, so they began to appoint other ministers to be pastors in their name. Among the ministers the bishop had available to appoint (ordain) to this task were his own deacons, who knew him and his ministry better than anyone. These close associates of the bishop were ordained to serve as priests, rather than deacons, and eventually (around the eighth century), the order of deacons became, at least in the Latin Church, a temporary or *transitional* stage that a man went through on his way to ordination as a priest.

In the last sentence, I used the expression *the Latin Church,* and this probably needs some further discussion. It is important to remember that in the early days of the Church, Christian communities were often quite small and very diverse with regard to language, customs, culture, and even religious expression. *All* of these Churches were in communion with the pope. To this day, there are more than twenty Churches that together comprise what we know as "the Catholic Church." The part of the Church with the most members is known as the "Roman Rite" or the "Latin Church." However, there are millions of *Eastern* Catholics as well — Catholics who are members of one of the many Eastern traditions of Catholicism. With regard to deacons and the diaconate, many of the Eastern Catholic Churches maintained a tradition of permanent deacons, while in the Latin or Roman Church, it had evolved into the transitional order described above. The Second Vatican Council asked that the permanent diaconate be restored in the Latin Church and renewed where necessary in the Eastern Catholic Churches.

The diaconate today exists in both forms. Seminarians who are preparing for eventual ordination as priests are still first ordained deacons, and since the Second Vatican Council, we also have so-called permanent deacons who remain in the order of deacons. In short, the diaconate did not disappear; it has simply taken on a different form and function.

6. Who are some famous deacons through history?

There are a number of well-known deacons. One of the most famous is St. Francis of Assisi (1181–1226), although a surprising number of people don't realize that he was a deacon. As a deacon, Francis was well known for his homilies, for his outreach to the poor and especially to lepers, and for his quest for "Lady Poverty." Francis believed that all that we have comes from God and rightly belongs to God; if we would find perfect holiness, we should return everything to God, seeking not merely to serve the poor, but to be poor ourselves. This radical approach to poverty was not well received in Francis's own day, but even now, a true Franciscan model of spirituality calls others to just such a radical conversion. Like all Christians, deacons find in Francis a powerful witness to discipleship; as a brother deacon, Francis offers an especially apt model of diaconal service. His feast is celebrated on October 4.

St. Lawrence (martyred in AD 258), a deacon of Rome, is perhaps less well known than Francis, but among deacons he's a giant. After his bishop was martyred (Pope St. Sixtus II), Lawrence was ordered by the Roman authorities to surrender the wealth of the Church. He returned a few days later with the poor of Rome, telling the Roman officials that the poor were the true treasure of the Church. He was led off to be roasted on a gridiron. Legend has it that while he was being burned, he told his executioners to turn him over since he was done on that side!

During the Jubilee Day for Deacons in February 2000, the relics of St. Lawrence were brought to the Paul VI Audience Hall at the Vatican. They were enshrined there throughout the day's events, including an address by the Holy Father. Every speaker made reference to the witness to *diakonia* given by St. Lawrence. Let's consider a few reasons why he is seen as a model deacon.

First, notice his relationship to his bishop. Lawrence was well known to the Christian community and to the Roman authorities as the bishop's primary assistant, especially where the care of the poor and the administration of the Church's goods were concerned. Second, notice that the authorities expected him to have access to the Church's wealth. Deacons have traditionally been associated with the temporal goods of the Church and as administrators; Lawrence is a good example of this. Third, Lawrence rightly demonstrates that the primary responsibility of the Church (led by the Church's deacons) is to the poorest and most marginalized of all. On every level—relationship to the bishop, administrative responsibilities, and care of the poor— Lawrence models the diaconate to us today. We celebrate his feast day on August 10.

There have been many other notable deacons: St. Ephrem of Edessa (d. AD 373) was well known for his asceticism, his catechetical work, his religious poetry, and his learning. Pope Benedict XV proclaimed him a "Doctor of the Church" in 1920, meaning that his scholarship and his way of life were so exemplary that they have had a significant influence on the Church. His feast day is June 9th. Reginald Pole (1500–58) was a member of the English aristocracy who was renowned for his learning and leadership. While still just a deacon, he was made a cardinal, and then appointed a papal legate who presided over the first session of the Council of Trent in 1545. In 1549 he reportedly came within one vote of being elected to the papacy. He was finally ordained a priest in 1556; two days later he was ordained a bishop and became the Archbishop of Canterbury until his death in 1558.

You may be wondering why I have not mentioned St. Stephen, the first martyr of the New Testament, who is often listed as a deacon, along with six companions in Acts 6:1–6. Although since ancient times this selection of the Seven has been considered the founding of the diaconate, none of these seven men is ever called a "deacon." However, for centuries, the Seven have been seen as diaconal in their ministry; they were ordained to restore communion

within a divided Jerusalem Christian community. Two of their number, Stephen and Philip, are then presented to us as great preachers
and catechists. Stephen was so effective and prophetic in his preaching that he enflamed the authorities and he was stoned to death.
Philip was led by the Spirit to catechize an Ethiopian official; after
he baptized this official, Philip was again whisked off by the Spirit
to catechize others. We celebrate the feast of St. Stephen on
December 26; St. Philip's is celebrated on June 6.

Through our history, then, we find deacons bringing people
together and to Christ, serving as preachers, teachers, administrators of the Church's goods, and martyrs. Deacons today are filled
by the same Spirit at their ordinations to fulfill the same roles in
the contemporary Church.

7. In the early Church, why were deacons often elected to become bishops?

Since deacons were the chief administrative assistants to the
bishops, they had the opportunity to experience the bishop's ministry "up close and personal." They knew what was on his mind and
in his heart, and they had a good sense of the local church from the
bishop's perspective. Therefore, it often made perfect sense to ask
the deacon to take on the office of bishop. This practice stopped, for
a number of reasons, in approximately the sixth century.

8. What were "archdeacons" and why did bishops have them?

As dioceses grew in size, sometimes a bishop would ask one
of his deacons to assume even greater responsibility and serve as
his primary assistant on almost every matter. One writer[8] has suggested that if we want to know what an archdeacon did, we should
look at what a vicar general and a diocesan chancellor do now (and
I would add the office of chief financial officer as well), and then
combine them into one person: That was what the archdeacon did.
The archdeacon often exercised juridical authority, would conduct

official visitations to parishes to examine pastoral practices and revenues, and carried out a wide assortment of other duties. As time passed and deacons were being ordained to the priesthood, the office of archdeacon remained, but it was filled most often with a priest. Eventually the office itself died out, especially as more modern legislation created specific offices (such as vicar general, chancellor, and chief financial officer) to take care of the archdeacon's functions. It's interesting to note that the term "archdeacon" still exists in other churches. For example, in the Episcopal Church, a person who is the director of the Office of Deacons is often referred to as an archdeacon.

9. After all these centuries, what led the Council to restore the diaconate as a permanent order of ministry?

The idea to renew the diaconate came from many parts of the world during the preparation periods prior to the Second Vatican Council. But the epicenter of the movement was in Germany. Beginning in the nineteenth century, some German Catholics began discussing the advantages of having the diaconate restored as a permanent order, just as it had been in the ancient Church. These discussions picked up steam in the early years of the twentieth century, especially after the devastation during and following World War I.[9]

What really drove the proposal to revive the diaconate, however, was World War II. The horrors of that war led many church leaders to discuss how the Church needed to be renewed to be a more effective witness of Christ to the modern world. Such conversations took place among the priest-prisoners incarcerated at the Dachau Concentration Camp. There they discussed what the Church might do to prevent more tragedies like those that had ravaged the first half of the twentieth century: world wars, worldwide economic depression, the rise of totalitarian regimes, and the *Shoah*. Soon these same men would see the beginning of the atomic age and the cold war.

Many possibilities were discussed, among them the insight recovered out of the horror of the concentration camp itself: that the Church herself was a *servant* and that the Church needed to respond to her own diaconal nature. A sacramental diaconate, lived as a permanent state of ordained ministry, could help restore that sense of service throughout the Church. Deacons would have a mission from their bishop to be leaders in service to the Church and the community; they would also have a responsibility to enflame and inspire the rest of the members of the Church to serve others as well.

Following the war, survivors of Dachau wrote about their experiences and insights.[10] A young man named Hannes Kramer of Freiburg, Germany, was inspired by these writings, and in 1951 he formed the first "diaconate circle" of men and women devoted to providing direct social service to those in need, as well as beginning research into the possibility of restoring the diaconate as a permanent order. The "diaconate circle" movement spread and attracted the attention of many postwar theologians, especially Karl Rahner, who began to write about the diaconate as a permanent order.

During an address to the Second World Congress of the Apostolate of the Laity in Rome on October 5, 1957, Pope Pius XII acknowledged the growing interest in the possibility of a renewed diaconate. Although he believed that the idea "at least today is not yet ripe," he encouraged bishops and theologians to continue their research into the "permanent" diaconate.[11] Before the Second Vatican Council actually began, hundreds of bishops from around the world requested that the revived diaconate be a topic of discussion during the Council. Thus the stage was set for the decision of the Second Vatican Council.

10. Exactly how did the Second Vatican Council "renew" the diaconate?

The bishops discussed the diaconate in conjunction with their discussions about their own role as bishops. While deacons are mentioned in several documents of the Council, it is in paragraph #29 of *The Dogmatic Constitution on the Church (Lumen Gentium)*[12] that the Council expressed its desire that the diaconate be renewed as "a proper and permanent" order of the hierarchy.

This decision on the part of the bishops of the Council was then implemented by Pope Paul VI in 1967.

11. What exactly does Vatican II say about deacons?

Paragraph #29 has two parts. The first describes deacons as ministers who are ordained "not for the priesthood, but for the ministry": "Strengthened by sacramental grace, they are at the service of the people of God in the ministry of the liturgy, the word, and charity, in communion with the bishops and his priests." Then a number of specific duties are listed, ranging from solemn baptism to presiding at funeral services and funerals. Most commentators agree that this list is not meant to be exhaustive, and that deacons may serve in many other capacities than those listed here, at the discretion of their bishops. What is most important here is that the deacon shares in the threefold apostolic ministry of Word, Sacrament, and Charity. We will examine these more closely a bit later.

The second part of the paragraph describes the diverse functions of deacons as "supremely necessary for the life of the church," and then decreed that the diaconate "can be restored as a proper and permanent grade of the hierarchy." It would be the responsibility of the various conferences of bishops (like the United States Conference of Catholic Bishops) to decide with the approval of the pope "whether and where it is opportune for such deacons to be appointed for the care of souls." Finally, the bishops established that the diaconate shall be open to married men "of mature age" (later established in canon law as thirty-five), as well as celibate younger men.

Pope Paul VI implemented this decision in 1967 with the document *Sacrum Diaconatus Ordinem*, and soon the bishops of

Germany, France, Belgium, Brazil, and parts of Africa received approval to restore the diaconate in their countries. The first ordinations took place in Germany and Cameroon in 1968. The bishops of the United States received approval in 1968, and the first permanent deacon in the United States was ordained in 1969. Now there are close to 14,000 permanent deacons in the United States out of nearly 30,000 around the world.

12. Paragraph #29 of *The Dogmatic Constitution on the Church* says that "strengthened by sacramental grace, [deacons] are at the service of the people of God in the ministry of the liturgy, the word, and charity, in communion with the bishops and his priests." What does this mean?

There are several important points contained in this sentence. First, the ministry of deacons flows from their sacramental ordination. As we will see later, many of the functions of deacons may be exercised by lay persons or priests, but the sacramental basis and the sacramental significance of the deacon's functions flow from his ordination. Second, deacons are at the service of the people of God. This means that deacons serve *all* of the Church and act in the name of the Church. Third, deacons serve in a balanced and integrated threefold ministry of Word, Sacrament, and Charity. We will discuss this ministry in greater detail a little later; for now what is most important is to stress the "balanced and integrated" nature of the ministry. According to *Permanent Deacons in the United States: Guidelines on Their Formation and Ministry, 1984 Revision,* the deacon's ministries of Word, Sacrament, and Charity "are not to be separated; the deacon is ordained for them all, and no one should be ordained who is not prepared to undertake each in some way."[13] Finally, the ministry of the deacon is only properly understood within the context of the sacramental communion that exists between deacons and their bishop and between deacons and their collaborators in ordained ministry, the priests.

13. I thought that the Second Vatican Council promoted *lay* ministry. If that's the case, why is the Church promoting clerical forms of ministry at the expense of lay persons who could do the job just as well?

This is a wonderful question, and one that many people have asked. The answer, I believe, can help us come to understand the nature of *all* ministry in a more comprehensive way.

First, while Vatican II certainly did promote lay ministry both in the world and within the Church, it did so within the context of encouraging all forms of ministry, lay and ordained. As with most things Catholic, we try to see things in "both/and" categories rather than "either/or" categories whenever possible! The Council saw *all* ministry, both lay as well as ordained, as a participation in the ministry and life of Christ. Second, this question seems to conceive of ministry as a purely functional matter; notice its assertion that the lay faithful "could do the job as well." As we have seen, however, there is more to ordained ministry (or anyone's ministry, for that matter) than simple function. The question presumes that all ordained ministry is simply about function; what's more, those functions are understood solely in terms of priestly ministry.

The fallacy of this understanding is easily seen if we tried to say the same thing about the priesthood. If someone were to say that there is no need to ordain anyone to the priesthood because qualified lay persons could be appointed to say Mass and hear confessions, we would quickly realize that this is not an adequate response. In our Catholic understanding of sacramental theology, we have come to understand that ordination to the priesthood has a sacramental meaning that goes beyond the specific functions of the priest. As a result of ordination, we realize that there is more to "being" a priest than simply "doing" priestly things. Similarly, then, ordination to the diaconate involves more than simply doing the "functions" of the deacon. We can begin to see that there is more to "being" a deacon than simply "doing" diaconal things.

The question also presumes that lay ministry somehow stands in opposition to the ordained ministries. This is another one of those "both/and" versus "either/or" situations. Of course we need lay ministry throughout the Church and especially *in* the world, the primary place for lay ministry. The Church, under the leadership of the laity, exists in the world as the "soul and leaven" (*Gaudium et Spes*, 40) of society.[14] But we also need a variety of ordained ministries. Ministry is a tapestry; we need all the threads to appreciate the richness and diversity of the whole, and each of those threads leads us to Christ.

Finally, the question does not take into account the development of the proposal to renew the diaconate in Germany and elsewhere prior to the Second Vatican Council. The proposal did not emerge from a shortage of priests or from an attempt to "overwhelm" the laity. Rather, when that history is considered, one quickly realizes that the diaconate was seen as complementing priestly and lay ministry; it was recognized for the radical nature of *diakonia* (a Greek word most often translated as "service") that the diaconate offers the Church. *Diakonia* is much more than simple menial service, however. It is a ministry of reconciliation, of outreach to the most marginalized and those most in need of care, education, and justice. The history of the diaconate shows that the revived diaconate was never intended to usurp the functions of the priesthood or to overwhelm lay ministry; it was to add its own unique sacramental character to the diaconal nature of the Church. This was a component of the vision of the survivors of Dachau, and it was this vision that most strongly influenced the vision of the bishops at Vatican II, who clearly saw the necessity of collaborative coresponsibility of all ordained and lay ministries for the common good of the Church and her mission.

14. If the Council wanted to stress the permanent nature of the diaconate, why are seminarians still ordained deacons before they are ordained to the priesthood?

In order to answer this very simple question, a bit of history will be helpful. Although the practice began much earlier in some parts of the Church, from about the eighth century clerics commonly moved upward from one order to another, normally culminating with their ordination as priests. This "coming up through the ranks" was known as the *cursus honorum* (literally, "the course of honors"), and it was modeled on what might be termed the "civil service" of the time. Until 1972 in the Latin Rite of the Catholic Church, this meant that a man would enter the clerical state through a rite called *tonsure,* which involved cutting the hair of the new cleric as a public sign of his commitment to the Church. ("Tonsure" comes from a Latin word meaning "to clip." If you have ever seen *Robin Hood* or other movies set in the Middle Ages, you've probably noticed the rather distinctive haircut worn by friars, monks, and clergy: the ring of hair with a bald spot shaved on the crown of the head. This distinctive haircut was, in fact, their tonsure). The rite of tonsure, which was not an ordination, made a person a cleric. As a member of the clergy, he was then eligible for ordination, and he would pass through the four minor orders known as *porter, lector, acolyte,* and *exorcist,* and then the three major orders of *subdeacon, deacon*, and *priest.* This was the established pattern for well over a millennium, and it was only revised in 1972 when Pope Paul VI, following the desires of the Second Vatican Council, eliminated the rite of tonsure and suppressed the minor orders and the major order of subdeacon. Today a person becomes a member of the clergy upon ordination as a deacon, and the only bald spots are the ones that occur naturally!

Even with the renewal of the diaconate as a permanent order, no longer solely a stop on the way to the priesthood, and even with the considerable restructuring within the sacrament of orders itself in the Latin Rite (the Eastern Catholic Churches still celebrate tonsure, the minor orders, and the subdiaconate), it remains the practice today that seminarians for the priesthood are ordained first to the diaconate. Following several months to a year as a deacon, they are then ordained to the priesthood. This is known as the "transitional" diaconate, although sacramentally this is inaccurate. Ordination always affects the one ordained *permanently*. When a "transitional" deacon is later ordained to the priesthood, he does not *cease* being a deacon, any more than a priest later ordained a bishop *ceases* being a priest. So, although some deacons later become priests and bishops, they remain deacons as well.

The practice of ordaining transitional deacons is coming under scrutiny by contemporary theologians. First, while the diaconate is a vocation related to the priesthood through the shared sacrament of holy orders, it is at the same time a vocation *distinct from* the priesthood. Deacons are not ordained to a kind of subordinate version of the priesthood; rather, they have their own unique nature and mission in the Church. With the renewal of the permanent diaconate, the former model in which clerics came "up through the ranks" until they were eventually ordained priests has been replaced. In short, the diaconate is no longer seen as an order that finds its sacramental significance in eventual ordination to the priesthood.

Second, in former years, the transitional deacon would often be assigned temporarily to parish ministry while completing his seminary formation. This was to be a type of "on-the-job" training, if you will, in which the soon-to-be priest was able to preach, celebrate some of the sacraments, and begin a gradual acclimation to priestly ministry in a parish. However, in today's programs of priestly formation, this kind of parish experience is done long before the seminarian is ordained a deacon. Therefore, the only experience most seminarian-deacons have of diaconal ministry is the essentially liturgical ministry they perform within the seminary or while at home on vacation from the seminary; hardly the same scope of diaconal ministry as lived and exercised by permanent deacons.

All of this, then, leads to the danger of a mistaken perception that there are really two diaconates: one transitional and one permanent. While sacramentally a permanent deacon and a transitional deacon are "equal," the lived reality is of two completely different states of life. For example, transitional deacons wear the clerical collar, while in most dioceses permanent deacons do not. For the transitional deacon, all of their activities are geared, focused, and directed toward their future identity and ministry as priests; not so with permanent deacons. While seminarians are given experience in various charitable and pastoral settings, this is not done as an essential element of their diaconate, but of their future ministry as priests. Even when they do serve in parishes, transitional deacons are often presented to the parish as soon-to-be priests, not within the context of their ordination as deacons. I was once assigned to a parish that enjoyed the services of a transitional deacon over the summer. He was asked by the pastor to give a homily during all of one Sunday's liturgies on his "Journey to the Priesthood." This he did, describing the diaconate as the last stage of his formation before his "true" ordination as a priest. I was also assisting at the Mass. After Mass, the pastor and the other deacon and I were greeting the departing parishioners. I was asked repeatedly when my own ordination (to the priesthood) was going to take place. On a different occasion my wife was asked by a parishioner, "When you die, will the deacon become a *real* priest?" It is no wonder that many people (including some priests) have an inadequate understanding of the true nature of the diaconate as a *permanent* state of ordained ministry.

As we have seen, there is only one Order of Deacons. Some theologians are beginning to suggest that since the vocation of the seminarian is properly to the priesthood and not to the diaconate, and because a transitional diaconate no longer seems to be serving the real pastoral and practical needs of the people of God, the practice should be discontinued. There is an even deeper reason offered. The primary reason the diaconate was renewed, as we have seen, was not simply for the benefit of the individual deacon, but to help the whole Church understand her diaconal role. The Second Vatican Council, and especially Pope John Paul II, has stressed this point, such as when the pope referred to the diaconate as a permanent order that "sacramentalizes the Church's own service." If this conciliar and papal vision is ever to reach its full potential, these theologians suggest that retaining a vestige of the *cursus honorum*—in which all ordained ministry is to be interpreted and finds its fulfillment within the priesthood—is an anachronism that ought to be stopped.

However, other theologians argue that continuing this practice still has a benefit in introducing the seminarian to the experience and diaconal nature of ordained ministry. Certainly, whether the Church continues to ordain transitional deacons or not is within her authority to adjust or adapt, just as was done with tonsure, the minor orders, and the subdiaconate. We will just have to see what judgments are made in the future.

15. So deacons and priests are ordained by bishops. Who ordains bishops?

This is a very good question, especially since it gives us a chance to discuss briefly what it means to be a bishop in the first place, and that is important when studying the diaconate. In fact, it is very important to understand the nature and role of the bishop if we want to understand the whole idea of ordained ministry in the Church. While this book cannot treat the subject in a comprehensive way, a brief description is necessary in order to see the nature and role of deacons in the proper context.

To answer the question directly and simply, a bishop is normally ordained by three other bishops, primarily as a sign of the communion that exists between the world's bishops. By virtue of their sacramental ordination, bishops form an "episcopal college" with the pope—as a bishop himself (the bishop of the Diocese of Rome)—at the head of that college. Through his ordination, a bishop possesses the fullness of apostolic ministry in all of its priestly and diaconal dimensions. The bishops at the Second Vatican Council put it this way:

> Episcopal consecration also confers the offices of teaching and of governing together with the office of sanctifying. (These, however, of their very nature, can be exercised only in hierarchical communion with the head and the members of the college.) For from tradition...it is clear that, by means of the imposition of hands and the words of consecration, the grace of the Holy Spirit is so conferred, and the sacred character so impressed, that bishops in an eminent and visible way undertake Christ's own role as Teacher, Shepherd, and High Priest, and that they act in his person. Therefore it devolves on bishops to admit newly elected members into the episcopal body by means of the sacrament of orders....One is constituted a member of the episcopal body by virtue of sacramental consecration and by hierarchical communion with the head and members of the body.[15]

The bishop has two sets of responsibilities. On the one hand, he is the pastor of the diocesan church he serves; on the other, because of his membership in the "college of bishops," he has a share in the responsibility of governing the universal Church. I think most people understand in general terms how a bishop cares for the diocese, but they often don't realize his universal responsibility. Once again, let's see what the Second Vatican Council teaches:

> The order of bishops is the successor to the college of the apostles in teaching authority and pastoral rule....Together with its head, the Roman Pontiff, and never without this head, the episcopal order is the subject of supreme and full power over the universal Church....[16]

This universal authority of the bishops, always exercised in communion with each other and under the authority of the pope—and never apart from him—is expressed in many ways. Probably the most visible way would be through a general council of the Church such as the Second Vatican Council itself, in which the world's bishops gathered as pastors and teachers of the entire Church.

Finally, regarding bishops' authority within their own dioceses, the Council says:

> In any community existing around an altar, under the sacred ministry of the bishop, there is manifested a symbol of that charity and "unity of the Mystical Body, without which there can be no salvation." In these communities [dioceses], though frequently small and poor, or living far from any other, Christ is present. By virtue of Him, the one, holy, catholic, and apostolic Church gathers together....Bishops govern the particular churches entrusted to them as vicars and ambassadors of Christ.[17]

It is only against this backdrop of the sacramental identity of the bishop that we can properly understand the sacramental identity of priests and deacons. Bishops ordain priests and deacons to their "lesser" offices (since only the bishop has the "fullness" of the apostolic ministry) in order to assist the bishop in carrying out his responsibilities for the whole diocesan church. The most recent revisions to the rites of ordination have even been restructured to reflect this fact. "The structure of this book is changed in such a way that it begins with the Bishop, who has the fullness of the sacrament of Holy Orders, in order to convey more clearly the idea that priests are the Bishop's co-workers and that deacons are ordained for his ministry."[18] We shall discuss these relationships in more detail a little later.

16. You just said that bishops are "ordained." However, the word *consecrated* was also used in one of the quotes from Vatican II. Are *ordination* and *consecration* the same thing?

The two terms mean roughly the same thing in the sense we are using them here, although in a more technical sense there are differences. The term *ordination* refers primarily to the "ordering" of ministry and life in the Church. In the Church, everyone has a place; everyone belongs to an "order." I like to think of the Gospel accounts in which Jesus feeds the multitudes as a graphic example. All four Gospels tell us about this miracle; Matthew even has two accounts. But in the Gospels of Mark and Luke, we read that the people sat "in groups of fifties" (Luke 9:14) or "in groups of hundreds and of fifties" (Mark 6:40). In short, every individual in that vast throng was "ordered." Some theologians have suggested that through baptism we become part of the "order" of the baptized.[19] We also speak of the "Order of Catechumens" referring to those who are in the process of entering the Church. In more ancient times we even spoke of the "Order of Penitents" to refer to those individuals who had received forgiveness of their sins but were still doing acts of penance (which sometimes lasted for a year or more). In the Church, everyone has a place. Through the sacrament of orders, some of the baptized are brought into the Order of Bishops, others into the Order of Deacons, and others into the Order of Priests.

A *consecration,* on the other hand, involves a calling upon the Holy Spirit to make someone or something holy. At Mass, for example, at the consecration, the elements of bread and wine are transformed into the Body and Blood of Christ through the invocation of the Holy Spirit that precedes it (known by the Greek term *epiclesis*). Similarly, every ordination is also a consecration since it involves an invocation of the Holy Spirit to fill the whole Church and in a particular way those being ordained. This special prayer, which is said by the bishop after he has laid his hands upon the head of each of those being ordained, is referred to as the "Prayer of Consecration."

Prior to the Second Vatican Council it was common to hear of a priest being "consecrated" a bishop. This was because many people in the Church understood the bishop as sacramentally a priest who had been given greater jurisdiction over a part of the Church. Therefore, a bishop "ordained" others, but he himself was "consecrated." The Council, however, reminded us that the act of

becoming a bishop has its own sacramental character and that it is
through this sacred ceremony that a person enters into the Order of
Bishops and becomes part of the college of bishops referred to earlier. Therefore, since the Council, the Church has returned to the
more ancient practice of referring to *all* such ceremonies, including that of a bishop, as "ordinations." Each ordination—to bishop,
priest, or deacon—involves a configuration of the one being
ordained to Christ, who is the High Priest and Deacon for all.
Therefore, to speak of a person being "ordained bishop" is the pre-
ferred—and theologically correct—term.

17. Can deacons help with the shortage of priests?

While there are many things that deacons may do that can
assist in the pastoral care of the Church, they are *not* substitutes for
priests, nor are they some sort of restricted order of priests.
Furthermore, the diaconate was not renewed by the Second Vatican
Council because of a shortage of priests. It has been said that the
Council did not restore the diaconate because of a shortage of
priests, but because of a shortage of deacons. While deacons have a
responsibility for some of the same things that priests do, deacons
have a different set of responsibilities that are unique to them, and to
try to use deacons as substitute priests would be a disservice to both.

We face many challenges when experiencing a shortage of
priests. The temptation is to focus on the functions of the priest to
see who else might carry some of them out *until we have enough
priests again.* Since certain diaconal functions (which will be discussed in more detail in chapters five through seven) are similar
to those of the priest, it is appropriate that deacons fully exercise
these ministries, whether there is a shortage of priests or not. In a
similar way, lay persons are called to certain facets of official
ministry that is theirs by virtue of their sacramental initiation. As
with the deacon, lay persons should be exercising their rightful
ministries, whether there is a shortage of priests or not. If the
Church experiences a shortage of priests (and this is not the first

time the Church has not had enough priests), then she must find ways of encouraging, nurturing, and enabling vocations to the priesthood, thereby respecting the integrity and identity of all the sacraments involved. Deacons as well as laity have authentic, legitimate, and necessary ministries *in their own right* that are not, dependent on a lack of priests for their exercise.

18. The deacon in my parish works selling life insurance. If deacons are clergy, why do they still hold regular jobs?

Although they are ordained, deacons most often serve within the framework of work and family life. On a practical level, deacons are responsible for providing their own livelihood for themselves and their families. They most often do this by remaining engaged in whatever job, career, or profession they were engaged in prior to ordination. (In my own case, for example, I was an active-duty Navy Commander.)

In addition to this practical consideration, there was a deliberate intention by the bishops at Vatican II to increase the official presence of the Church in the secular world. In the words of one of the Council's participants, Cardinal Karol Wojtyla, later Pope John Paul II, "A particularly felt need behind the decision to restore the permanent diaconate was that of a greater and more direct presence of sacred ministers in areas such as the family, work, schools, etc., as well as in the various ecclesial structures."[20] In some cases, deacons leave their secular employment and, if they have the appropriate qualifications, pursue a compensated full-time position within the Church.

19. Are you saying that, when all is said and done, most deacons are just part-time ministers?

Nothing could be further from the truth! Ordination is something that affects a person *permanently,* so being a deacon is not a part-time ministry. Once ordained, the deacon is always a deacon, regardless of where he is or what he's doing, just as a priest or bishop is always a priest or bishop even when they're on vacation.

Since deacons are often employed and have families, some people only see the deacon "doing ministry" when he's engaged in some activity at the parish. However, this highlights a very important point: Ministry in the Church is not something that happens only within a church building, during a church-sponsored activity, or at liturgy. A deacon is just as engaged in his ministry when he is at work or engaged in other activities not directly related to the Church. It is precisely in his leadership and presence *outside* formal ecclesial structures that the deacon can often enable and empower others to exercise their own diaconal responsibilities as Christians. Being a deacon is a full-time reality!

Two

The Formation of Deacons

Deacons likewise must be serious, not double-tongued, not indulging in much wine, not greedy for money; they must hold fast to the mystery of the faith with a clear conscience. And let them first be tested; then, if they prove themselves blameless, let them serve as deacons.

First Letter to Timothy 3:8–10

20. What sort of training and formation do deacons receive?

There is an intense period of discernment and formation for those who are considering life as a deacon. Standards for this process have been established by Church (known as "canon") law, policies from the Holy See (the formal term referring to the "See of Peter": the Pope and his advisors), the appropriate national bishops' conference (in this country the United States Conference of Catholic Bishops in Washington, DC), and the local bishop. While there is great flexibility in diaconate formation, several important factors apply to all.

Canon law (that is, the system of laws that govern the Church) states that a married man may be ordained a deacon at age thirty-five; an unmarried man may be ordained at age twenty-five.[21] However, the USCCB has decided that *all* candidates for the permanent diaconate should be thirty-five. The local bishop can waive one year from this requirement, and if the bishop would like to ordain someone even younger than thirty-four, he may request authority to do so from the Holy See.

Being a deacon involves a vocation from God; it is not simply another job or ministry that a person may volunteer for. Therefore, a man goes through an intense application and screening process. Should the bishop determine that the person might have a vocation to the diaconate, he may admit the man into a formal period of discernment, called *aspirancy*. During this period of prayer, study, and personal formation, the man and his family (if married) reflect on the nature of ordained ministry and whether this is something that the man might be called to. Following aspirancy, the bishop may decide to admit the man into formal *candidacy* for ordination. This is *not* a guarantee of eventual ordination: It simply means that the bishop is asking the man to pursue additional human, spiritual, academic, and pastoral formation in order to further discern a possible vocation. This period of formation is particularly intense, involving significant coursework in theology, scripture study, homiletics, church history, and so on. In most parts of the world, including the United States, diaconate formation may last from three to six years or more, depending on the process put in place by the bishop. In the United States, the current average length of diaconate formation is about four years.

Following this period of formation, the bishop reviews the candidate's entire record and progress of discernment. If the bishop deems it appropriate, and only with the formal, written consent of a married candidate's wife, the bishop may call the man to ordination. Following ordination, deacons—like priests— are required to continue their formation through annual retreats and regular ongoing formation opportunities.

21. How does someone know if he has a vocation to be a deacon?

There is a maxim that says "Grace builds on nature." In many cases, a person's diaconal qualities have been observed and experienced by friends, family, and members of a parish community; in these cases, it is often some of these people, or a pastor, who suggest to a man that he ought to consider the possibility of the diaconate. Perhaps a man has become interested in the diaconate because of his own experience with deacons or through something he has read. In every case, a person who thinks he might have a vocation to the diaconate should first pray, then talk about it with his family, if he's married, and find out more by calling the director of the diaconate for the diocese in which he lives.

The entire formation process is also a journey of *discernment*. Through the systematic opportunities for prayer, spiritual direction, formal course work, and pastoral-skills development afforded by the formation experience, the candidate is able to reflect critically on his life and the various vocations to which he might be called. This process of discernment continues up to the very moment of ordination.

22. Are there special courses to take to become a deacon?

Yes, there certainly are. The formation of deacons involves four essential dimensions: the human, the spiritual, the intellectual, and the pastoral. As you can see, the intellectual (or academic) dimension is just one of the four elements of formation; all four are required. When we focus on the intellectual preparation needed for the diaconate, however, we find that deacons study the same subjects that other ministers do: theology, scripture, preaching (known as homiletics), church history, and so on. Since most deacon candidates are employed outside the church, and most of them are also married with family responsibilities, these courses are offered in the evenings or on the weekends.

The courses are designed in a variety of different ways, usually determined by the resources available in the diocese. For example, if there are Catholic institutions of higher learning in the diocese, some of the courses might be offered there, using existing programs and faculty. In other cases, a faculty of qualified instructors is assembled, and specific courses unique to the diaconate are designed and taught. Some programs incorporate elements of distance learning, and still others bring instructors into the diocese to conduct the formation sessions. Every diocese develops its own specific and unique approach to diaconate formation.

23. Do deacons all have college degrees in theology?

There are no specific academic prerequisites for deacons established in universal Church (canon) law or, in the United States, by the United States Conference of Catholic Bishops. A few bishops have decided that having a degree in theology or religious studies is important for effective ministry in their dioceses, and have established that as a local requirement.

Based on the most recent information available, about 58 percent of deacons have college degrees: 30 percent have bachelor's degrees and another 28 percent have graduate degrees. It is important to realize, however, that not all of these degrees are in theology. Most candidates come to the formation process with their formal education behind them, which means they may have degrees in any field; in some ways, this is part of the great diversity that is found in the diaconate. Another 26 percent of deacons have had some college, 15 percent have high school or GED diplomas, and about 1 percent have less than a high school or GED diploma.[22]

24. With this diversity in educational background, how does the bishop make sure that a person is well prepared for professional ministry as a deacon?

The formation of deacons is a complex process. First, there is a very selective application and interview procedure before a person can even begin the formal discernment process. If a person is admitted to the program, there is a period of aspirancy during which the man (and his wife, if he is married) find out more about the diaconate and spend considerable time praying and reflecting on whether God might be calling the man to this ministry. If everyone agrees that there might be a vocation present, then the bishop *might* call the aspirant into formal candidacy. This is an intense period of preparation during which discernment continues together with the various dimensions of formation. Only when the bishop is comfortable that there is a vocation to the diaconate and that the candidate has demonstrated overall competence to serve as an effective deacon, does he call the man to ordination.

Throughout the entire process of aspirancy, pre-ordination formation, and ongoing formation after ordination, there are four dimensions that must be present.[23] Developed from the 1981 Apostolic Exhortation *Pastores Dabo Vobis* ("I Will Give You Shepherds") concerning priestly formation, these four dimensions are the human, the spiritual, the academic (or intellectual), and the pastoral. As you can see, the academic formation of a deacon candidate is only one of the four required dimensions. There are national standards established by the United States Conference of Catholic Bishops that help each diocesan formation program ensure that their candidates for the diaconate are well prepared and competent for the rigors of the ministry.

25. I always thought that members of the Catholic clergy had to be celibate. Why can a married man be a deacon?

Although celibacy—that is, a solemn promise to remain unmarried—is valued as an important gift to the Church, it is *not* an inherent or essential part of being ordained. In the early days of the Church, many, if not most, Catholic ministers were married, the most obvious example being St. Peter himself. (Remember the famous Gospel passage in which Christ cures Peter's mother-in-law?)[24] Over time, clerical celibacy became the norm in the Latin Rite of the Church; in the Eastern Catholic churches, however, married clergy continued to be, and indeed, is still the norm.

When pastoral ministers and theologians began to discuss the renewal of the diaconate as a permanent order prior to, during, and after World War II, the possibility of ordaining married men as deacons was widely accepted and anticipated. This was not out of a desire to threaten priestly celibacy; rather, it was based on the fact that deacons are *not* priests. Furthermore, many of the people already serving in diaconal roles (although still not ordained) were married, and it was understood that deacons would be serving within a different cultural and ecclesial context than priests. Since the revival of the permanent diaconate, most deacons and their families attest to the mutuality of the sacraments of matrimony and orders. While the mutuality of the charism of celibacy and orders has been well documented in the Latin Rite, it has been a genuine blessing to rediscover the shared gifts of marriage and orders.

In the case of married candidates for the diaconate, the Church requires that the wife freely consent to the ordination of her husband. If there are any unusual circumstances within the family situation of the deacon that would hinder the effectiveness of the person in ministry, or if it is determined that the demands of ordained ministry would be too disruptive to the family, the bishop will not call the man to ordination.

26. You mentioned that the bishop decides whom to ordain; however, does a person just volunteer to be a deacon?

No, becoming a deacon is much more than just volunteering; seeking ordination to any Order is not about personal desires and ambition. Sometimes a person's pastor or family suggests the diaconate as a possibility; in other cases, a person has felt an interest in the diaconate and approaches diocesan authorities to find out more about it. In every case, however, those who apply are scrutinized carefully as to their overall human, spiritual, academic, and pastoral qualifications, experience, competence, and potential. This process of intense and rigorous discernment continues throughout formation. What is important to remember is that a person becomes a deacon *not* out of personal desire or interest, but only for the common good of the Church as determined by the bishop. That is why the selection, discernment, and formation of deacon candidates are so rigorous and intense.

THREE

LIVING LIFE AS A DEACON

Preach the Gospel always; use words if necessary.
St. Francis of Assisi, Deacon

27. How does a deacon balance family, job, and ordained ministry?

Very carefully! Most married people already understand the importance of balance in their own family relationships; becoming a deacon adds another set of relationships into the equation. It is never a question of one set of relationships being more important than another: All of them are critical, and sometimes one relationship takes precedence over another. It might be helpful to consider a married person who is on a business trip for a week. That person doesn't stop being married, with all of the responsibilities that being married entails, but for that week, the person's job takes precedence. This is similar to the kind of balance that is necessary in the deacon's life. Once ordained, he accepts responsibilities that cannot be set aside lightly, any more than he can set aside the responsibilities arising from marriage.

In the diaconate community, we used to hear quite often that a deacon's priorities were first to his relationship to God, second to his wife and family, third to his employer (since he can't very well do much of anything if he's out of work), and fourth to the diaconate. While this makes sense in a carefully qualified way, it runs the risk of reducing the diaconate to a set of functions that the deacon may or may not do, and only after his responsibilities to the first three priorities are fulfilled. The reality is much more complex. This kind of balance can be achieved only by constant prayer and by exceptional communications skills between the deacon and his wife, employer, bishop, and other partners in ministry.

28. Given all of this responsibility, wouldn't it just be better to wait until retirement to become a deacon?

Absolutely not! The whole vision of the diaconate is that of a person engaged with the world as well as the Church. This is not to minimize the wisdom and experience of older candidates for the diaconate, whose children may be grown and who may be retired from their secular jobs, who bring these gifts to the service of the Church. However, one of the driving forces behind the renewal of the diaconate was to have the presence of ordained ministers in the workplace, the marketplace, and the family. Here in the United States there has been a tendency for possible candidates to "put off" the question of the diaconate until later in life. This may be seen in a couple of simple statistics. In Germany the average age of a permanent deacon is about forty-one. While data on the age of deacons in other countries is sketchy, it does seem that this is fairly consistent around the world. On the other hand, the average age of a permanent deacon in the United States is about sixty-one. This suggests that in the United States, more men are deferring the possibility of a vocation to the diaconate until later in life. When the Second Vatican Council considered the diaconate, however, there was never a thought that it would be a ministry exercised by men who had already raised their families or completed a secular career. Rather, the deacon was perceived as an experienced minister who was actively engaged in the life and ministry of the Church and the world.

It is important to remember that we are talking about a vocation from God. Sometimes younger men considering the diaconate are advised (even by deacons!) to wait until their children are grown and they have more time to give to formation and ministry. On the surface that may seem like a reasonable response. However, now consider our response if we were approached by a young man who expressed interest in a possible vocation to the priesthood. We would most likely encourage this person to begin a process of discernment immediately; we would probably not insist that he wait until he retired from a secular profession first.

To defer a vocation to the diaconate until a person "has more time" implies that a deacon's ministry is something focused on parish and liturgical activities. While this is partially true, the deacon is intended to provide a unique witness in the marketplace and the family; he is an ordained, official presence of the Catholic Church within the broader community. The vocation of the deacon is to be an ordained presence of Christ the Servant in the world. This is something that a younger person can do with great energy and enthusiasm.

None of this is meant to suggest that there is not much to be gained from the hard-earned wisdom of older candidates. Furthermore, the intense formation involved truly is a challenge for a younger candidate with responsibilities for a young family and a secular job, career, or profession. Nonetheless, deacons of any age must learn to juggle and balance multiple responsibilities; one's ability to do this becomes an important aspect of discernment and formation. The bottom line here is that younger candidates need to be encouraged, and it should not be presumed that, simply because they are younger, they and their families will be unable to do what is necessary. Such automatic deselection based on age does a disservice to the prospective candidate, his family, and—ultimately—the Church. The proper place to test the possibility of a vocation is within the application, selection, and discernment process of the formation program itself.

29. I understand that priests receive a salary for their ministry. Do deacons get paid, or are they volunteers?

In general, deacons are not compensated for their ministry as deacons. Sometimes a deacon holds a job in the Church as a member of the bishop's staff or as a parish employee, such as the principal of a parish school. In these cases, the deacon is usually paid whatever a lay person would be paid for serving in the same position. Notice that such compensation is associated with the position accepted by the deacon in addition to his ecclesiastical assignment as deacon, for which no compensation is generally provided.

The bishop of a diocese may also establish norms for the reimbursement of expenses incurred as a result of service as a deacon: mileage, for example, or the cost of liturgical vestments.

Most dioceses provide a modest allowance to help defray the costs of continuing formation and an annual retreat.

30. What happens if a deacon decides to leave active ministry?

A deacon, just as a priest, might leave active ministry in a number of ways. Once ordained, of course, the deacon remains a deacon forever, just as a priest remains a priest forever, regardless of how one leaves the ministry. That said, a deacon might simply *retire* from active ministry due to age or for health reasons. Many dioceses have established retirement ages, usually around the age of seventy or seventy-five, for all of its clergy.

A deacon might leave active ministry on a *leave of absence.* This is generally a temporary situation in which the deacon needs some time away from ministry to focus on personal or family issues that demand considerable attention and energy. A deacon who is caring for an elderly parent, for example, might take a leave of absence until the situation is resolved. At the end of the leave of absence, the deacon would normally return to active ministry.

A deacon might be *suspended* from ministry. In this case, suspension is a punishment for a violation of canon or civil law. For example, if a deacon were to try to hear confessions and give sacramental absolution, which is something reserved to priests and bishops, his bishop would probably suspend him from ministry. A suspension is lifted only when the bishop is confident that the behavior will not take place again.

Finally, there is a *formal dispensation from the obligations of clerical ministry.* This is sometimes incorrectly referred to as "laicization," or "being returned to the lay state." This is not accurate since, as said above, "once ordained, always ordained." What happens in this case, however, is that the cleric receives a formal and permanent release from the rights and obligations associated with the clerical state. This process can be initiated by the deacon or priest, or by his bishop or religious superior, for a variety of reasons. Sometimes a cleric discerns that he should no longer function in official ministry; in other cases, the cleric may have committed a grave offense that makes it inappropriate for him to serve in ministry any longer. Whatever the cause, this action results in a permanent release from the rights and obligations of ordained ministry.

31. Deacons often minister in the world, and so do lay persons; are they doing the same things?

This is true on occasion, but the fact that deacons and lay persons sometimes do exactly the same things is an important indicator that the real significance of the diaconate lies not in what deacons *do,* but in who they *are.* Sometimes we might think of ordination as a ceremony in which a person is given the authority to do certain things that other people cannot. For example, after a man is ordained a priest, he can "say Mass" and "hear confessions." The day before ordination, he couldn't do either!

In the case of the deacon, however, there are no real clearcut differences. There are certain liturgical actions that the deacon performs (such as proclaiming the Gospel), but in most cases, deacons and laity do very many of the same things. Here's the difference: The deacon, as an ordained minister, has a permanent and a public responsibility for a ministry of Word, Sacrament, and Charity. What's more, through ordination, he becomes an icon of Christ the Servant; when a person sees the deacon, it is hoped that the person will see and experience Christ at work in the world. The deacon also speaks and acts as an official representative of the Church and is responsible for a faithful presentation of the fullness of Church teaching and mission. As a baptized Christian, he is called to be a disciple of Christ in the world, as are all Christians; as an ordained deacon, he is called to a share of the apostolic ministry. As such, he is a leader of the community, especially with regard to the Church's own *diakonia.*

32. The deacon is a member of the clergy, but he usually lives and works among the laity. How should a deacon relate to the laity?

The deacon should be a collaborator, a friend, and, sometimes, a challenge! St. Augustine once said in a sermon, "For you I am bishop, with you I am Christian. The first is the title of the office I received, the second is by grace; the first implies danger, the second salvation."[25] This could easily be paraphrased to apply to priests and deacons as well. "For you I am deacon, with you I am Christian...." The deacon should be a minister that is particularly effective at helping people see the connections in their lives between the Gospel and the implications of the Gospel in everyday life; furthermore, the deacon should be a prophetic witness to all concerning the people most in need of the community's care and concern.

Let's examine this paraphrase more closely: "For you I am deacon" — ordained ministers exist to serve the baptized (not the other way around); "an office I have received" — deacons serve the baptized in an official capacity as a representative of Christ and the whole Church; "the first [the title of deacon] implies danger" — serving as deacon is dangerous because it requires deacons to make themselves vulnerable, and to sacrifice themselves at the service of others; as leaders, deacons are to be visible prophets of the Lord, something that is often not popular with those who hear the prophecy; "the second salvation" — through it all, however, deacons are fellow disciples, graced to follow Christ through whom they hope to find salvation.

33. I once heard a diocesan official say that our diocese wants to focus on developing priestly vocations and lay ministry, so we don't need deacons. Is this comment accurate?

No, unfortunately, it isn't accurate. The simple fact is that ministry in the Church and in the world is a tapestry of many colors, and we need all of them for the tapestry to be as vivid and beautiful as it might be. The diaconate adds a particular nuance, a singular focus to ordained ministry that is complementary to priestly ministry and lay ministry. The general experience of most dioceses since the diaconate was renewed in the United States in 1968 has been that an environment that encourages *all* lay and ordained ministries results in an increase in vocations to all ministries. One researcher has described the situation in this way:

> Dioceses with proportionately more permanent deacons also have higher priestly ordination rates. If two dioceses have identical values for the other variables in the model but Diocese A has 20 more permanent deacons per 100 active diocesan priests than Diocese B, every three years Diocese A will have approximately 1 more priestly ordination per 100 active priests than Diocese B. Perhaps whatever diocesan conditions account for a flourishing permanent deacon program also promote more successful recruitment to the diocesan priesthood.[26]

In other words, most dioceses have learned that it is not necessary or good stewardship to prefer one vocation over another. There is sometimes concern that the costs associated with promoting the diaconate along with lay ecclesial ministry would be prohibitive and that a choice needs to be made between them. The reality is, however, that with reasonable planning and good collaboration and sharing of resources, this need not be the case. The lesson learned in most dioceses has been that the benefits of a comprehensive approach to ministry formation, both lay and ordained, far outweigh the costs.

34. Can women be ordained as deacons?

At this time women are not ordained to the diaconate. As most people realize, Pope John Paul II has taught that the Church does not have the authority to ordain women to the priesthood.[27] It is not clear whether the specific teaching of this document applies to deacons as well; the Church has not taught *definitively* on the subject of the possibility of the ordination of women to the diaconate. When approached on this very question, the head of the Congregation for the Doctrine of the Faith at the Vatican, Cardinal Ratzinger, responded that the possibility of ordaining women as deacons remains a question open for debate and discussion. Some theologians hold that, because of the essential unity of the sacrament of orders, it would be impossible to ordain women to the diaconate; other theologians argue that, even within the essential unity of the sacrament, sufficient diversity exists to distinguish between the sacerdotal (priestly) orders of bishops and presbyters, and the order of deacons. Because of this diversity, they argue, it might be possible to ordain women deacons.

It is unlikely that women will be ordained to the diaconate any time soon. However, it is important to recognize that the discussion of such a possibility does not fall into the same category as proposing the ordination of women to the priesthood. Unless and until the official teaching authority of the Church determines otherwise, the topic of women deacons remains open for discussion and debate.

35. I have heard that there were *deaconesses* in the ancient Church. Who were these women, and were women ever ordained as deacons?

There are two groups of women associated with the diaconate in the ancient Church. It would appear that some women, such as Phoebe (see Romans 1:1), were deacons, although we don't really know what that might have meant at that point in history. Certainly in the case of Phoebe, St. Paul refers to her as a *diakonos* (the Greek word from which we get the English word *deacon*), using a masculine form of the word, not a feminine form. This has led some commentators to suggest that he was using the word *diakonos* as a title, just as we might today.

A short time later in history we encounter a group of women known as "deaconesses," and they seem to be a distinct group from the "deacons." Whereas Phoebe was referred to as *diakonos* (and we don't know too much more than that) these women were referred to in the feminine as *diakonissae* and we have some record of their liturgical "commissioning." There is scholarly debate over whether this was an actual ordination or some other sort of commissioning ceremony[28] The role of the deaconess was to assist with the baptism of female catechumens and other types of ministry in which it was more appropriate for women to minister to other women. In the case of catechumens, for example, baptism was still done by full immersion, and it was deemed far more appropriate for another woman to be in the pool with a female catechumen than for a male deacon, for obvious reasons.

Modern Christian churches that ordain women seem to prefer the term *deacon* over *deaconess;* in such churches, such as the Church of Sweden or within the Anglican communion, there is no functional distinction made between deacons who are men and deacons who are women.

36. Do deacons get transferred from parish to parish like priests?

Yes, deacons may be transferred, because when a person is ordained a bishop, deacon, or priest, he is at the service of the entire diocese, not just a particular parish or ministry. Therefore, from time to time, depending on the needs of the diocese, deacons are transferred to a different assignment. Sometimes bishops will do this on a regular schedule; at other times transfers are requested by deacons, priests, or pastors. The essential point here, however, is that *all* the ordained are ordained to meet the needs of the entire diocese, and the bishop is responsible for putting the right "talent" to meet the needs in the best location.

This process of reassignments is, of course, made somewhat more complicated by the fact that the vast majority of deacons are married. This does not change the basic rationale for assignments or reassignments; it merely means that the deacon's family and professional responsibilities are considered in the development of the details of the assignment. Married or celibate, the deacon remains a diocesan minister, subject to the assignment of his bishop.

37. A deacon in a neighboring parish was just elected a judge. I thought Catholic clergy weren't supposed to be involved in politics, so why was he able to do this?

Church law (canon 284, §3) forbids most clerics from entering public life, but it also *exempts* permanent deacons from this prohibition (canon 288). This underscores the fact that deacons have a unique leadership responsibility for service in the community. So, while it is the unique vocation of the laity to transform culture, the deacon is the Church's own representative to be with and to serve the laity; the deacon should provide leadership, inspiration, and challenge to the laity as they carry out the responsibilities of their own baptisms. Since in most cases the deacon himself is still involved in everyday responsibilities of job and family, his leadership by example can be particularly effective.

In some cases, this leadership may take the form of public service. With the consent of his bishop (and only with his consent), the deacon may enter various forms of public life, such as running for elective office or serving on boards and other civic endeavors. This approval of the bishop is essential, however, since the deacon has a responsibility to the bishop and the entire Church. If there is something in his past or in the nature of the office he is seeking that might bring discredit or scandal to the Church, the deacon should not (and his bishop will probably insist that he not) pursue the office. I should also point out that transitional deacons (those who are ordained deacons prior to eventual ordination as priests) are bound by the canonical prohibition from entering public life.

38. Why do some deacons dress like lay persons, and others wear the white clerical collar that I normally see priests wearing?

A little context is in order. In the earliest years of the Church, clergy wore *no* distinctive garb. Over time, and for a wide variety of reasons, the development of a manner of dress that would identify a person as a member of the clergy or as a member of a religious order took hold. It is important to point out that there has never been an absolute standard for clerical dress, even to this day. There are different customs between the various churches (Eastern and Western) of the Catholic Church, and even in the Latin Rite there is considerable variation. For example, in many academic settings, priests on the faculty often wear jackets and ties; at other schools, priests wear clerical attire.

In the last paragraph, we spoke of "clerical" garb; notice that this applies to *all* clerics, not just to priests. That means that, until 1972, one began wearing clerical attire once admitted to the clerical state with tonsure (the special haircut), and through the whole sequence of the minor and major orders. The white clerical collar so common today is technically appropriate for all those who have been ordained: deacons, bishops, and priests. However, there is a popular misunderstanding that "the collar" is the exclusive attire of *priests:* Transitional deacons wear the collar because they are going to become priests, and bishops wear the collar because they are also priests. It is this common misperception that only priests (including priests-in-training) wear the collar that has led to considerable confusion. The "clerical collar" has been transformed into the "priest's collar."

Church law (canon 284) requires that *all* clergy wear "suitable ecclesiastical garb according to the norms issued by the conference of bishops and according to legitimate local customs." However, canon 288 includes this canon in a list of things that "do not bind permanent deacons unless particular law establishes otherwise." Therefore, among all the clergy, only permanent deacons are relieved of the obligation to wear clerical garb under universal law. The diocesan bishop or the national conference of bishops may establish *particular law* governing the use of clerical attire; however, in the United States, the United States Conference of Catholic Bishops has chosen not to establish a particular law on this matter for the dioceses of the United States. The bishops prefer that each diocesan bishop be free to determine what the best pastoral practice is for his diocese. Some dioceses forbid their deacons from wearing the clerical collar because they are afraid people might confuse deacons with priests (although transitional deacons wear the collar, and most people seem to have no trouble determining if they're priests or not). In other dioceses, deacons may wear the collar at their discretion whenever they are involved in public ministry, or in certain circumstances determined by the bishop. For example, the bishop might insist that his deacons wear the clerical collar whenever serving in a jail or prison environment. In still other cases, deacons wear a clerical shirt that is of a different color than black, while the priests of the diocese are directed to wear *only* black shirts.

Some deacons are concerned that, without some sort of easily recognizable garb that identifies them as clerics, people will not know that they are deacons and available to serve. With priests, people see the collar and respond accordingly; conversely, without the collar, deacons sometimes have trouble identifying themselves as members of the clergy to others. Since many ministers of other churches also wear some sort of clerical attire, this complicates matters even further. I was once assigned to serve at a prison as a member of chaplaincy team that included priests and Baptist and Lutheran ministers. The priests and ministers all wore clerical collars. In this case, I also wore the collar since the bishop in this diocese wanted deacons to wear collars when serving in prison ministry. However, in other dioceses, the practice might be different, and the only minister associated with a chaplaincy who is *not* easily identifiable by his attire is often the Catholic permanent deacon.

Other deacons and their bishops find that wearing a clerical collar puts too much distance between the deacon and the people he is to serve. For them, the collar becomes less of a tool of identification than a barrier to ministry. It is this great diversity of opinion and experience that leads to such varied practices between dioceses. The United States Conference of Catholic Bishops says simply that "in exceptional circumstances, a diocesan bishop, with due consideration for the practice of neighboring dioceses and with appropriate consultation, may decide that deacons should wear some distinctive garb when engaged in formal clerical ministry."[29] Notice the "exceptional" nature of such a provision. The general understanding and preference is that deacons ought to resemble the people they serve.

39. What other clerical obligations does Canon 288 address for permanent deacons?

Under canon law, deacons generally have the same rights, responsibilities, and obligations as other clergy (that is priests and bishops). However, canon 288 exempts permanent deacons from several of these obligations. I have already mentioned the exemption of permanent deacons from the obligation of clerics to wear clerical attire (canon 284), or their exemption from the requirement to refrain from secular public office. Canon 288 also exempts permanent deacons from the obligations of canons 285, §§ 3 and 4; 286; and 287, §2. Let's look at each of these briefly.

Canon 285, §1, states that "clerics are to refrain completely from all those things which are unbecoming to their state, according to the prescripts of particular law." Deacons are bound by this paragraph, as are all other clerics. Notice that this canon does not say these unspecific things are evil in themselves; simply that they are "unbecoming" or inappropriate for clerics. The former *Code of Canon Law* (promulgated in 1917) listed a few examples, such as bartenders, jailers, and taxi-cab drivers. The new *Code* does not give specific examples and leaves it up to the judgment of the cleric and those concerned with particular law. Canon 285, §2, is similar in nature, except that it forbids clerics (including deacons) from activities "which, although not unbecoming, are nevertheless foreign to the clerical state." Again the older *Code* had specific examples, such as practicing medicine or surgery. By not including such specific examples, the 1983 *Code* again leaves the specific application of this paragraph to the judgment of the cleric and particular law. I have discussed these paragraphs (which *do* bind permanent deacons) so I can contrast them with the next two paragraphs of the canon, which do *not* bind deacons.

We have already seen that Canon 235, §3, states that clerics are forbidden "to assume public offices which entail a participation in the exercise of civil power." Since canon 288 exempts permanent deacons from this canon, a deacon *may* assume such public offices, which would include any number of elective or appointed offices that exercise public authority. The United States Conference of Catholic Bishops, however, has provided a strong caution on this point: "While the *Code of Canon Law* permits permanent deacons to hold political office, a deacon should consult with his bishop before seeking or accepting such an office. In particular cases, the bishop may forbid such an undertaking."[30]

Canon 285, §4, states that clerics are not to manage the goods of lay persons or of secular offices "which entail an obligation of rendering accounts." They are not to "give surety even with their own goods" and they are to "refrain from signing promissory notes, namely, those through which they assume an obligation to make payment on demand." Throughout the canon, clerics are told that if they are going to do such things, they must first consult with their "Ordinary" (usually that term refers to the diocesan bishop) and receive his prior permission. This canon includes responsibilities such as being the executor of an estate, guardian of minor children, and so on. Given canon 288, however, permanent deacons may do these things.

Canon 286 prohibits clerics from "conducting business or trade personally or through others, for their own advantage or that of others." Canon 287, §2, prohibits clerics from having "an active part in political parties and in governing labor unions unless, in the judgment of competent ecclesiastical authority, the protection of the rights of the Church or the promotion of the common good requires it." Permanent deacons are exempted from both of these canons.

Probably the simplest way of looking at these various canons is to understand that the Church is attempting to keep her ordained ministers from an *excessive* involvement in secular affairs. Leadership in society and culture, and the transformation of secular structures and institutions, is more properly and appropriately the role of the laity. What makes the provisions of canon 288 so interesting, therefore, is that the Church is consciously removing such restrictions from her permanent deacons. Of course, deacons are not to usurp the rightful obligations of the laity in the world, but there is an acknowledgement that deacons themselves live in the world and can actually serve as an official presence of the Church in these various pursuits. Such involvement naturally involves great discretion, prudence, and balance so that the interests of all are protected.

40. People refer to bishops as "Bishop" or "Your Excellency." We call our own priest "Father." What do we call deacons?

Most deacons prefer to be called simply by their first names. If they have a professional title (such as doctor, professor, or a military rank), it is, of course, appropriate to refer to the deacon by this title in professional matters. In the context of the Church, it is always appropriate to address a deacon as "Deacon" followed by his first or last name.

Transitional deacons (those who are in the seminary preparing to be ordained to the priesthood) are referred to as "Reverend Mister." There has been some confusion about whether permanent deacons should be referred to in the same way. On the one hand, there is only one Order of Deacons, whether one is a permanent or transitional deacon. This would imply that all deacons should be referred to in the same way. Therefore, in some dioceses, *all* deacons are referred to as "Reverend Mister." Other bishops prefer to keep the title "Reverend Mister" reserved for transitional deacons, and they refer to their permanent deacons simply as "Deacon." (One bishop once told me that he personally objected to this practice, saying that we do not refer to priests as "Priest Smith" or "Priest Jones.") Still other bishops are concerned that "Reverend Mister" combines a clerical title ("Rev.") with a secular title ("Mr."), thus perpetuating the myth that deacons are not truly ordained, or, as some people put it, that they are somehow "lay deacons"—which is a misnomer. So these bishops refer to all of their deacons—permanent or transitional—as "Reverend." To confuse matters even more, it is the practice of the Eastern Catholic churches to refer to their deacons as "Father Deacon"!

Such inconsistency of practice only adds to the confusion over the true nature of the deacon and the meaning of the deacon's ordination. These seemingly superficial issues of dress and address betray some of the underlying ambiguity that persists about the diaconate. Most deacons long for the day when a consistent practice will emerge on all of these related issues: what deacons are to wear or not wear, what deacons are to be called, and so on. The confusion impedes service and distracts from far more important pastoral matters, and deacons simply want to get on with the ministry.

Such confusion over such a simple question! Here's the simple answer: "Deacon" is always appropriate.

Four

The Relationships of the Deacon

Whoever wishes to be great among you must be your servant, and whoever wishes to be first among you must be your slave; just as the Son of Man came not to be served but to serve, and to give his life a ransom for many.

Matthew 20:26–28

41. I thought deacons worked for priests; what is a deacon's relationship to the bishop?

In parish life, it is easy to assume that the deacon "works" for the pastor, since the pastor has overall pastoral responsibility for the parish, and this includes the supervision and support of all clergy assigned by the bishop to the parish. However, from a theological and historical standpoint, in fact from the very earliest mention in scripture, deacons have been most closely associated with their bishops. This is still the case. During the ordination of a bishop, all of the attending bishops lay their hands on the head of the new bishop; during the ordination of a priest, all the attending priests lay their hands on the head of the new priest. However, during the ordination of a deacon, *only* the bishop lays hands on the head of the new deacon. Furthermore, on certain occasions, such as ordinations, bishops may wear the dalmatic (a sleeved tunic) of a deacon under his chasuble, demonstrating his own sacramental identity as a deacon as well as priest and bishop.

In very many cases, the deacon is assigned to work in a parish setting at least for part of his ministry. This means that he is responsible to the pastor, just as any other clergy (such as a parochial vicar or another priest residing in the parish) is responsible to the pastor. What is important to remember, however, is that ultimately a priest or deacon's authority to function in ministry comes not from the pastor of a parish, but from the bishop of the diocese.

As we saw earlier, in the ancient Church deacons were said to be the "eyes and ears, heart and soul" of the bishop, and deacons still have that special relationship to their bishop today. Recently, Pope John Paul II wrote that "the Bishop will seek in every way possible to know personally all the candidates for the diaconate. After their ordination he will continue to be a true

father for them, encouraging them to love the Body and Blood of
Christ whose ministers they are, and Holy Church which they
have committed themselves to serve...."[31]

42. What does the bishop expect from his deacons?

I was once privileged to be a speaker at a diocesan gathering of permanent deacons and their wives, along with a number
of the priests of the diocese. Toward the end of the day, the diocesan bishop joined the gathering. Standing in the center of the
room, surrounded by his deacons, the bishop began his remarks
by saying, "When I ordained you, you assumed an obligation to
share the concerns of my heart for the pastoral care of this diocese. Today, let me share what is on my heart, so that it may be on
your hearts, too!" The insights of this bishop are profound, and
capture the essence of the relationship that should exist between
the bishop and his deacons. Furthermore, we can see what the
bishop expects from his deacons: that they share in his own apostolic ministry to care for the people of his diocese.

First and foremost, therefore, the bishop should expect his
deacons to understand his responsibility for the entire diocese and
to understand that their responsibility is to help the bishop
throughout the diocese. In the early days of the renewed diaconate, some deacons and priests, and perhaps even some bishops, thought of a deacon as being a *parish* minister rather than a
diocesan minister. Gradually and fortunately, this understanding
is giving way to a clearer appreciation of the diocesan scope of
the deacon's responsibility.

Second, the bishop should be able to expect his deacons to be
competent across the full spectrum of diaconal functions: ministers of the Word, ministers of Sacrament, and ministers of Charity.
Deacons cannot simply choose one or two functions that they will
perform and disregard the rest. This threefold office should be
fully integrated into the ministry and life of the deacon, and the
deacon is expected to be competent in all of them. Notice that

"competence" does not mean that every deacon must try to be a new Fulton Sheen in his preaching; it does mean, however, that he understands the purpose of liturgical preaching and can be effective in doing it. Similarly, no one can be an expert in every type of social justice ministry. Some people do better in prison ministry than hospital ministry; others do better in bereavement ministry than they do in counseling couples for marriage. Nonetheless, the deacon must be able to handle situations competently.

Finally, the bishop should expect his deacons to be operating on the fringes of society, preaching the good news and being in contact with those people no one else will touch. At a recent statewide gathering of more than five hundred deacons and wives, one of the bishops in attendance was asked how he saw the diaconate being used in his diocese over the next five to ten years. The bishop replied that there was a particular geographical region in his diocese that had almost no Catholics and, in fact, was well known for its anti-Catholic attitudes. The bishop announced that he had decided to "let loose the deacons" into that region, and he hoped that within five to ten years, the Church would be thriving there. This bishop's decision to "let loose the deacons" shows a great appreciation of the sacramental identity of the deacon as envisioned by those who brought the idea of a renewed diaconate to the table at the Second Vatican Council.

43. I know the bishop is a priest, but is he a deacon, too?

Yes. The bishop, according to the Second Vatican Council, has received the fullness of apostolic ministry through his ordination as bishop. This would naturally include priestly and diaconal dimensions. In a very real sense, the first deacon of any diocese is Christ. As a vicar of Christ, the bishop is also deacon to his diocese, and the deacons serving in that diocese are sharing in the bishop's own diaconate.

More concretely, under our current sacramental system, all bishops have been ordained to the diaconate as well as to the presbyterate (priesthood) prior to their ordination into the episcopate.

44. In our diocese, a couple of our deacons are in charge of diocesan offices. Don't these offices have to be held by priests?

Prior to the Second Vatican Council, most Catholics were accustomed to seeing priests in almost every aspect of church life. Some priests, for example, spent their entire priestly ministries as teachers in schools and were never assigned full-time to a parish. In other cases, priests spent most of their time as administrators or diocesan officials, even when, technically speaking, the position did not necessarily call for a priest.

Prior to the new *Code of Canon Law,* which went into effect in 1983, several important diocesan offices *had* to be filled by priests. However, the revised *Code* eliminated some of those requirements. Officials known as the *vicar general* (the diocesan bishop's chief deputy) and the *judicial vicar* (the head of the diocesan court on behalf of the bishop) must still be priests. But most diocesan staff positions may now be held by qualified lay women, lay men, members of religious congregations, and deacons.

45. What are "faculties," and why does a bishop give them to deacons?

One source defines faculties as "grants of jurisdiction or authorization made by church law or by a competent superior to perform ministerial acts such as hearing confessions, officiating at weddings, granting dispensations."[32] In other words, "faculties" describe the specific authority a priest or deacon has to exercise certain functions, and all priests and deacons must have faculties from the diocesan bishop. For example, if a deacon moves from one diocese to another, he will need to request faculties from the new bishop in order to function on a regular basis in the diocese.

A deacon's faculties normally include functions such as celebrating baptisms, weddings, funerals, and prayer services; proclaiming the Gospel and preaching at Mass and other occasions; and performing other functions described in canon and liturgical law.

46. Since the bishop has priests, why does he need deacons?

The bishop needs both priests and deacons, because their ministries are different. As was said before, deacons are not ordained simply to help priests or to fill in where there are shortages of priests. Therefore, even though deacons may at times exercise some of the same ministries as priests, they still retain their own unique set of ministries as well, and the bishop needs both in his pastoral care of the diocese. Even more fundamental, the deacon is a sign of Christ the Servant within the community, just as a priest is a sign of Christ the High Priest. Cardinal Walter Kasper has written that priests and deacons are like "the two arms of the bishop."[33]

47. Why do some bishops have deacons and others do not?

The vast majority of the dioceses of the United States do have deacons in ministry. Some bishops, however, have been reluctant to restore the diaconate in their dioceses for any number of reasons. Some believe that by encouraging the diaconate, they might lose vocations to the priesthood; others believe that the diaconate might discourage lay involvement in ministry; still others believe that they do not have the resources necessary to provide adequate formation for deacon candidates. As mentioned earlier, however, some studies have shown that a climate that encourages vocations to ordained ministry results in greater vocations to all ministries, and that one does not siphon off interest in another. Nonetheless, it remains the right and obligation of the diocesan bishop to determine how best to meet the needs of his diocese.

48. The bishop has a special sacramental relationship with his priests and a similar sacramental relationship with his deacons. So, what is the deacon's relationship with priests?

I've already quoted Cardinal Walter Kasper's wonderful image that deacons and priests are like "the two arms of the bishop."[34] This captures the kind of complementary partnership that should exist between deacons and priests. Both deacons and priests receive their authority to function in ministry through their sacramental ordination and the faculties extended to them by the bishop. Truly they are partners and brothers in ministry.

49. If the deacon and the pastor can't get along, can the pastor "fire" the deacon?

Only the bishop can assign and reassign the deacon; it is the responsibility of the diocesan bishop to make all assignments of clergy within the diocese. The deacon has been ordained by the bishop and assigned to specific duties; clearly it is the expectation that the deacon will be exercising those ministries to the fullest extent. Should the relationship between a deacon and his pastor deteriorate to the point where they cannot collaborate, they should communicate this fact to the bishop so that appropriate steps can be taken.

Short of reassignment, the pastor is responsible for the pastoral life of the parish, and he does have the authority, at least on a temporary basis, to ask the deacon not to exercise certain functions (such as preaching, for example). This is not a good solution, however, since the assignment of the deacon to serve in that parish was not made by the pastor but by the bishop. If that assignment needs to be significantly modified or changed, the bishop is the appropriate person to do so.

50. If bishops are deacons, are priests deacons, too?

As mentioned above, the long-standing practice of the Church is to ordain seminarians (men preparing for possible ordination to the priesthood) to the diaconate as a final step prior to ordination to the priesthood. Therefore, all priests are also deacons, although once ordained to the priesthood, they no longer function as deacons, with one exception: During the ordination of deacons, they are presented with the book of the Gospels and told to "believe what you read, teach what you believe, and practice what you teach." It falls to the deacon to be the normal proclaimer of the Gospel. When a deacon is not present at Mass, the Gospel is then proclaimed by a priest; when this happens, the priest is actually exercising his diaconate.

It should also be noted that ordaining future priests to the diaconate is not theologically necessary. This practice developed during the rise of the *cursus honorum* described on page 25. You will recall that in that system, a person was ordained from one order to another until he was finally ordained a priest. That pattern was revised with the revitalization of the permanent diaconate and the promulgation of *Ministeria quaedam* in 1972. While some continue to believe that there is a benefit to ordaining transitional deacons, there is a growing concern that continuing this practice, in light of the renewed permanent diaconate, serves no pastoral purpose and is actually counterproductive. Certainly this is a practice that the Church could change with relative ease.

51. How do deacons and priests collaborate?

When I first considered this question, I was reminded of a quip attributed to Blessed John XXIII. A journalist once asked him how many people worked in the Vatican, and the pope responded, "About half of them!" The pope cleverly took a question about the quantitative number of workers and turned it into a qualitative response. Considering our current question qualitatively, one might ask how *well* deacons and priests collaborate, and since we are dealing with human nature, that is a complex reality! However, we want to deal primarily with more quantitative issues: In what areas might priests and deacons collaborate effectively?

Deacons and priests collaborate on many levels. Most often this collaboration is seen in parish ministry, although they also collaborate in many other areas of ministry as well: hospital and prison chaplaincies, diocesan service, even on national advisory boards and staffs. Collaboration is most effective when both priests and deacons realize their own unique areas of specialization and appreciate each other's gifts.

52. Are deacons "lower" on the hierarchical ladder than priests?

Until the *Code of Canon Law* was revised in 1983, a person could not be ordained to any order other than the priesthood without fully intending to proceed on "up the ladder" to the priesthood. With the restoration of the diaconate as a permanent order in the hierarchy, this "ascending ladder" of ministries is not really the best language to use any more. However, the idea of a minister coming up through the ranks of lesser orders still resonates with some people because it was in place so long (from about 800–1972) and because we still ordain transitional deacons on their way to the priesthood. And, even though Vatican II referred to deacons as being "at a lower end of the hierarchy," the bishops were still working from the older model of ministry.

A much more helpful description today would be to refer to deacons simply as a distinct order of ministry, one ordained "not unto priesthood, but to *service*."

53. Are priests "full-time" ministers and deacons "part-time" ministers?

Ordination to *any* order affects the person ordained in a permanent way. All ordained ministers are, theologically and canonically speaking, "full-time" ministers. This is an important point: A deacon is not just a deacon when he vests for Mass any more than a priest is just a priest when *he* vests for Mass. A priest on vacation in Hawaii is just as much a priest as a deacon working as a farmer in Iowa is a deacon. This concern, that deacons are "part-time" ministers, perhaps arises from an overemphasis on "functionalism," which is addressed on page 5 above. In the eyes of the Church, however, ministry does not just take place "in the church." Ministry, including the official ministry of the deacon, takes place in the world, the workplace, and the family. So even if a deacon can only be involved in parish-related activity for a few hours a week, that does not mean he is not a minister every minute of every day spent elsewhere. One of the main reasons to revive the diaconate was to take advantage of this very important point.

54. Can a deacon be the pastor of a parish?

Under canon law, *only* a *priest* can be a pastor. When there is a shortage of priests available for assignments as pastors, the bishop may appoint "a deacon, or a lay person, or a group of persons" (canon 517, §2) to provide daily pastoral care and leadership for a parish. When this particular canon was being prepared, the Code Commission noted that a deacon, due to his sacramental ordination, bears an "ordinary and permanent" responsibility for the pastoral care of a parish, even when no priest is present. Nonetheless, the circumstances surrounding the assignment of someone other than a priest to lead the pastoral ministries of a parish are "extraordinary" (literally, "out of the ordinary"), since the normal expectation and hope of the Church is that every parish community would be served by a resident pastor. As we have seen, only a priest may serve in such a capacity. Any other arrangement is extraordinary and, hopefully, temporary.

55. What is the relationship between deacons and priests assigned to a parish, other than the pastor?

In many ways, deacons and priests other than the pastor who are assigned to the same parish find themselves in very similar situations. For example, the other priests need delegation to witness marriages within the parish, just as the deacons do. Priests other than the pastor are also responsible to the pastor for the specifics of their pastoral ministry, and the pastor functions as their supervisor, just as he does for the deacons. This flows from the pastor's overall responsibility to the bishop for all aspects and dimensions of pastoral ministry, within the parish, and not because other priests or deacons are lesser ministers.

In today's environment in which most of our priests are serving as pastors, this distinction between priests who are pastors and those who are not is often lost. Certainly, the partnership of deacons with priests not serving as pastors can be most helpful and a source of great potential for collaboration.

56. How many permanent deacons are married?

The latest statistics available indicate that well over ninety percent (90%) of all permanent deacons worldwide are married.[35] An additional three percent are widowed. This is a consistent percentage around the world.

57. Are there celibate deacons?

There are three kinds of celibate deacons. First are the transitional deacons who are in the seminary preparing for possible ordination as priests. They make a promise of celibacy upon their ordination as deacons. Second are those permanent deacons who are single at the time of ordination. They also make a promise of celibacy at their ordination as deacons, and may *not* marry after ordination. The third category is that of widowed permanent deacons, men who were married at the time of ordination, but whose wives have since died. Normally, these men will continue in ministry as celibate deacons.

58. If the wife of a deacon dies, may the deacon get married again?

Canon law normally prohibits any cleric from getting married. Notice that canon law *does* allow married men to be ordained to the permanent diaconate; but normally, once ordained, a man cannot marry. This means that if a deacon's wife dies, the normal course is for the deacon to remain celibate. Under certain conditions, a deacon's bishop may petition the Holy See for a dispensation from canon law so that the deacon might marry again, but this is an exceptional situation and not the norm.

59. What is expected of a deacon's wife?

No married deacon may be ordained without the freely given, written consent of his wife. She is expected to participate in the formation program to the greatest extent possible. This will give her the best opportunity to grow in her knowledge of the diaconate and its possible impact on her and her whole family. This will not only allow her to give informed consent to her husband's ordination; it also encourages her own spiritual growth in discipleship.

In terms of official ministry, there is no specific role for the deacon's wife. Every wife—indeed every couple—will need to discern particular dimensions of ministry for themselves. The deacon's ordination does not confer any ministerial role to the deacon's wife. However—and this distinction is crucial—many wives of deacons have been deeply involved in their own right in ministry for many years prior to their husband's ordination. This should continue to the extent desired by the deacon's wife—not as an outcome of her husband's ordination, but flowing out of her own baptism. Some wives who have not been active in ministry become drawn to ministry as a result of the formation process.

Again, their ministerial involvement does *not* flow from their husbands' ordination.

There is no single model or paradigm for the wife of a deacon to follow. Some wives choose to be extremely active in ministry based on their own qualifications and interests; other wives prefer to remain engaged in activities not related to official ministry. Parishioners need to be sensitive to the needs and dynamics of the deacon's family, and not presume, simply because the deacon is married, that his wife must also be engaged in a public, official ministry. This puts unrealistic and sometimes inappropriate pressure on the wife and family.

60. Will a married deacon have time for much ministry?

Each deacon will find, in collaboration with his family, his employer, his pastor, and his bishop how the specific demands of his ministry will be met. There are many variables involved, and no one pattern will apply to all.

It is important to remember that once ordained, a deacon is always a deacon, even when involved in activities unrelated to church matters. This is one of the unique features of the diaconate: as a full-time minister, even when engaged in a secular occupation, the deacon extends the sacramental presence of ordained ministry into the secular realm.

While the deacon may have only limited time available for activities traditionally associated with ordained ministry within the life of the parish, his ordination means that he has become a permanent and public sign of Christ the Servant regardless of where he is and what he's doing. This is no different than what we understand of *priestly* ministry: priests are not priests only when they are exercising specific priestly functions. They are priests always and everywhere; so, too, deacons are deacons always and everywhere.

61. If a married man is ordained a deacon, do he and his wife have to refrain from sexual activity after his ordination?

Not at all! Married deacons and their wives do not surrender any rights or responsibilities resulting from their married state of life. Marriage and orders are *not* incompatible sacraments; rather, there is a great mutuality between them.

Since the experience of most Catholics in the Latin Rite has been to associate ordained ministry with celibacy, it can be somewhat startling to realize that an ordained minister is married. I was once assigned to serve as the deacon of a parish near a Navy base to which I was assigned. One Sunday, after assisting and preaching at several Masses, I was getting into our family car with my wife and our children. Later in the week, the pastor called me laughing to say that I had created quite a stir with a new, young parishioner. It seems that Father was giving this new parishioner an overview of the parish, including the staff and various ministries. He mentioned that there was a permanent deacon on the staff, and the young man asked if the deacon had been preaching the previous Sunday. When he found out that I had been the preacher, he told the pastor that he had seen me do something after Mass that was quite disturbing. When the pastor inquired further, the young man said that he had seen the deacon "getting into his car with a woman and *her* children," and that this just wasn't right. The pastor gently explained that I was a permanent deacon, married, with children. The young parishioner said, "Yes, I know deacons can be married, but…." It took him a while, but eventually the image of a married ordained minister became more familiar to him.

While theologians have long explored the relationship of celibacy to ordained ministry, they are just now beginning to examine the theological relationships between marriage and ordained ministry; much work remains to be done.

62. If the wife of a deacon dies, should the deacon become a priest?

As should be clear from what has already been said above, the vocation to the priesthood and the vocation to the diaconate are distinct. For this reason, a vocation to the diaconate does *not* indicate a vocation to the priesthood. A widowed deacon who believes he may have a vocation to the priesthood should enter into prayerful discernment in dialogue with the director of priestly vocations and the diocesan bishop. Any subsequent ordination to the priesthood of a permanent deacon should always be an exceptional instance.

63. What happens if a deacon and his wife get divorced? If that marriage is later annulled, may the deacon marry again?

First things first: If a deacon and his wife were to divorce, regardless of the circumstances, the bishop will first ensure that all members of the family receive appropriate pastoral care to deal with the issues involved. The bishop will also ask the deacon to take a leave of absence; in other words, the deacon will no longer function as a deacon for a time. This gives the deacon the time and the freedom to attend to his personal affairs and to the needs of his family without the demands of public ministry. This leave of absence will continue as long as necessary, and any decision regarding the deacon's return to active ministry should be made only upon careful reflection, study, prayer, and consultation with the diocesan bishop, any professional consultants necessary, and the deacon himself. The overall health of the deacon and all members of his family is paramount.

For purposes of this question, let us assume that the divorced deacon has now returned to active ministry and that his marriage has been declared null by a Church tribunal. In the case of a lay person, this would in most cases mean that the person is free to marry in the Church. However, as was mentioned above, canon law forbids a person already ordained from getting married. To do so, he would have to seek a dispensation from the Holy See. The same canon, of course, would apply in this case. However, the Holy See will look extremely carefully and cautiously at the case of a divorced deacon who is seeking to marry again. In theory, it may be a possibility; in practice, however, it will be extremely rare.

64. Is the family involved in a candidate's formation for ordination as a deacon?

As our experience with the diaconate grows, there has been a commensurate appreciation of the importance of the entire family to the formation of a married permanent deacon. In the early years of the revived diaconate, the assumption was frequently made that the ordination was only a matter of concern for the candidate himself. As years went by, it became quite clear that the involvement of the wife in the process was crucial. Now we are entering into a further realization of the importance of the entire family. The *National Directory for the Formation, Ministry and Life of Permanent Deacons in the United States,* approved by the bishops of the United States and awaiting final approval by the Holy See, stresses the importance of involving *all* members of the deacon candidate's family during the formation process.

FIVE

THE DEACON AS MINISTER OF THE WORD

Receive the Gospel of Christ, whose herald
you now are.
Believe what you read, teach what you believe,
and practice what you teach.
Rite of Ordination of Deacons

65. What exactly is the ministry of the Word, and what is the deacon's role in it?

The ministry of the Word, in its broadest sense, includes evangelization, catechesis, liturgical preaching, and the proclamation of the Gospel. During the Jubilee Day for Deacons, Pope John Paul II challenged deacons: "Dear deacons, be active apostles of the new evangelization. Lead everyone to Christ! Through your efforts, may his kingdom also spread in your family, in your workplace, in the parish, in the diocese, in the whole world!"[36] During his ordination the deacon is given the book of the Gospels by the bishop with the charge: "Receive the Gospel of Christ, whose herald you now are: Believe what you read, teach what you believe, and practice what you teach."[37]

Within the Eucharist, deacons ordinarily proclaim the Gospel and also, by virtue of ordination, "possess the faculty to preach everywhere."[38] In short, "the deacon is called to proclaim the Scriptures and instruct and exhort the people."[39]

66. Why does the deacon proclaim the Gospel at Mass, and not the priest?

One of the most traditional liturgical roles of the deacon has been the proclamation of the Gospel at Mass. Even when the bishop—or even the pope!—presides at Mass, it is the deacon's responsibility to proclaim the Gospel. This flows directly from the bishop's charge to the deacon during his ordination (see the previous question). The deacon is the appropriate and "ordinary" minister of the Gospel because the deacon can witness to the assembly the concrete nature of our response to the good news in our own lives and times.

67. What is the role of the deacon in preaching?

St. Francis of Assisi, himself a deacon, is reported to have told his followers to "proclaim the Gospel always; use words if necessary." By virtue of his ordination, the deacon has a particular responsibility for preaching, which is a sharing in the bishop's own preaching responsibility. It was envisioned prior to the Second Vatican Council that one of the deacon's primary functions would be preaching in the midst of the assembly.

Furthermore, the character of the deacon's preaching should reflect the uniqueness of diaconal ministry. The deacon should bring to his homilies a prophetic sense of the service to which all are called. Through his own experience with those most in need, the deacon has an obligation to proclaim the community's responsibility to those in need in light of the Gospel.

68. Why do some deacons never preach at Mass?

In the early days of the renewal of the diaconate, some bishops were reluctant to have their deacons preach on a regular basis, believing that preaching was a particular function of the priesthood. Therefore, in some dioceses here in the United States, deacons were not always trained in homiletics (the study of preaching), nor were they given faculties to preach. Furthermore, since preaching by deacons was seen by some in the United States as somehow restricted to priests, and since there was an understandable desire not to confuse the roles of priest and deacon, preaching by deacons was often discouraged and even minimized in some diaconate formation programs. Unfortunately, this still remains the case in some locations.

These points of view appear to be almost uniquely American, growing out of a rather functional approach to ministry that neglects many of the insights which led to the renewal of the diaconate at the Second Vatican Council. Historically, scholars have long debated whether preaching was considered an ordinary function proper to the deacon in the ancient Church. However, while we look to the ancient Church for many reasons, we are not bound to observe rigidly every detail of ancient Church life and practice. Whether deacons preached or not in the ancient Church is less important than the expectations of the contemporary Church as she has continued to grow under the inspiration of the Spirit.

As was seen earlier, preaching by deacons was seen as a critical and essential component of the deacon's role by those who pressed for its renewal at the Second Vatican Council. Building largely on the experience and expectations of the Church in Germany, the deacon was seen as having a mission from his bishop to seek out those in need and to return to the liturgical assembly and exhort and inspire the entire Church to live up to its baptismal responsibilities for the care of others.

As the experience of the renewed diaconate has grown, therefore, a deeper appreciation of the unique contributions of diaconal preaching has been gained. While deacons should not and need not preach at every Mass, neither should they *never* preach; as sharers in the bishop's own preaching ministry, they have an obligation to preach that must be respected, encouraged, and nurtured.

69. I am used to priests and bishops being teachers in the Church; however, are we now to consider deacons also as "official" teachers in the Church?

By virtue of their ordination, deacons share in the leadership and catechetical responsibility of the bishop. They do what they do both in the person of Christ and in the name of the Church; they *are* official teachers in and of the Church.

70. If a priest is going to give the homily at Mass, shouldn't he also proclaim the Gospel at that Mass instead of the deacon?

Deacons hear this question quite a bit, especially when they are serving in a parish that has not had the frequent or consistent service of a deacon. Let me respond with an initial observation. In all of the times we've seen the pope celebrate Mass on TV or perhaps even in person, we have never see him proclaim the Gospel at one of those Masses. Even at a papal Mass, it is *always* one of the deacons who proclaims the Gospel, regardless of who is going to give the homily. Proclaiming the Gospel is a ministerial function (as contrasted with a priestly function), and the Church has traditionally reserved this function, appropriately, to the deacon.

Second, there is nothing that necessarily "links" the Gospel alone to the homily. The homily is to reflect on *all* of the scriptures that have been proclaimed or on the significance of a particular feast or celebration. A homilist might just as easily decide to focus on one of the earlier readings or the Responsorial Psalm as from the Gospel itself. If that's the case and we were to follow the logic of this question, would the homilist suggest that he read the first reading or chant the psalm in order to connect them with the homily? Of course not. It is the same with the Gospel.

Sometimes, regrettably, the desire for the homilist to proclaim the Gospel is simply to save time during the liturgy. If the homilist proclaims the Gospel, there is no need to wait for the deacon to leave the ambo or pulpit and for the homilist to take his place. This is the least acceptable of all the possible reasons to adopt this practice.

Finally, it is important to remember *why* the deacon is the most appropriate minister to proclaim the Gospel. Through his ordination, the deacon is obliged by his bishop to be "the herald of Christ" and is presented with the book of the Gospels. The deacon, through his sacramental identity as a sign of Christ, who *is* the Good News and who came to pour out his life for the sake of others, is in a unique position to represent Christ in the midst of the assembly. All members of the assembly, be they pope or catechumen, baptized, priest, or deacon, receive this Gospel of sacrificial self-giving, and it is the deacon who is the sacramental sign of Christ the Servant.

71. What is the deacon's role in evangelization?

All the baptized are called to proclaim the good news of Jesus Christ; evangelization is an obligation of discipleship. In the *Dogmatic Constitution on the Church,* the bishops of the Second Vatican Council taught that through baptism, the faithful "must profess, before all, the faith they have received from God through the Church."[40] Furthermore, through the sacrament of confirmation, "they are more strictly obliged to spread the faith by word and deed."[41]

However, in addition to the obligations conferred by the sacraments of initiation, the ordained take on additional responsibilities for evangelization as a result of ordination. According to Pope John Paul II in his talk to deacons and their wives in Rome for the Jubilee Day for Deacons in 2000, deacons are "apostles of the new evangelization." An apostle is one who is "sent" (this is the meaning of the original Greek word *aposotolos*) by the risen Christ to proclaim the good news to all people. The deacon, as apostle, is sent on a variety of assignments and finds himself often in places and situations that most other clergy do not. It is precisely in these situations that the deacon's unique apostleship and official presence can be most powerfully felt. The deacon, by representing Christ and also his own bishop, can extend the good news through leadership, word, and example throughout all dimensions of human life.

Six

Deacons as Ministers of the Liturgy

Strengthened by sacramental grace, in communion with the bishop and his group of priests, deacons serve the People of God in the ministry of the liturgy, of the word, and of charity.

The Dogmatic Constitution on the Church, #29

72. Since deacons are supposed to focus on *service*, why are they involved in liturgical ministries anyway?

First, consider the importance of the liturgy, especially the Eucharist. The Second Vatican Council taught that the liturgy "is the outstanding means by which the faithful can express in their lives, and manifest to others, the mystery of Christ and the real nature of the true Church."⁴² Furthermore, "the liturgy is the summit toward which the activity of the Church is directed; at the same time it is the fountain from which all her power flows."⁴³ Finally, the Council reminded all of us that the Church "earnestly desires that all the faithful be led to that full, conscious, and active participation in liturgical celebrations which is demanded by the very nature of the liturgy"; in fact, this goal was to be considered "before all else" in the restoration of the liturgy.⁴⁴

Given these dramatic teachings of the Church about the centrality of the liturgy to the identity and life of all the baptized, we must always remember that our understanding of the liturgy should never be reduced to some sort of theatrical performance or series of liturgical functions. All of us, including deacons, find our spiritual and ecclesial identity expressed in and through the liturgy, especially the Eucharist. Deacons, therefore, have a unique role in the liturgy precisely as living signs of Christ the Servant.

Furthermore, there is a basic unity or integrity between the three dimensions of ordained ministry, so much so that the Second Vatican Council referred to all three as "service" *(diakonia)*. One leads to and nurtures the others. Ordained ministers are to model this basic, integrated relationship that should exist between Word, Sacrament, and Charity. Think of it this way: How often do we bemoan the fact that some people seem very religious or spiritual while at Mass, but then go out to the church parking lot and begin acting as if there were no connection between what went on inside the church building and what goes on outside? It is the role of the ordained, including the deacon, to help "connect the dots" and show that our teaching (Word), worship (Sacrament), and care and concern for others (Charity) are all part of the same reality: our relationship with God through Christ and the Spirit. When deacons are involved in the sacramental life of the Church, they are doing so as part of the much larger context of service to God and community.

73. What sacraments do deacons celebrate?

Current canon and liturgical law permits deacons to serve as ordinary ministers of baptism. ("Ordinary" in this sense refers to the fact that deacons exercise this ministry as a normal result of their ordination and the faculties they have received from the bishop. This is contrasted with "extraordinary" ministers who may baptize in an unusual emergency situation.) They are ordinary ministers for the distribution of communion (although, of course, deacons do not preside at the Eucharist itself). Deacons also officiate at weddings as the official witness of the Church (remember that in the Latin Rite, the *ministers* of the sacrament of matrimony are the *spouses* themselves). Deacons do *not* confirm, ordain, reconcile (that is "hear confessions" and give absolution), or anoint the sick.

In addition to these sacraments, deacons preach in virtue of their ordination, and they may also preside at various prayer services and liturgies, including Benediction of the Blessed Sacrament, public recitations of the Rosary, Stations of the Cross, the Liturgy of the Hours, and Sunday celebrations in the absence of a priest. While they do not celebrate the anointing of the sick, they are ordinary ministers of viaticum (holy communion given to those in danger of death); deacons may also preside at wakes and funerals.

74. Are there differences between when a priest baptizes and when a deacon baptizes?

There are no differences (other than perhaps a difference in presiding style or a preference of a different liturgical option) in any of the sacramental functions shared by deacon and priest. A baptism is the same, weddings are the same, and so are funerals and wake services.

75. Since deacons may baptize, may they also officiate at the sacrament of confirmation?

The normal ("ordinary") minister of confirmation, at least in the Latin Rite, is the bishop. Under certain circumstances the pastor may confirm, but the deacon *never* presides at the sacrament of confirmation.

76. If there is no priest present, may a deacon preside at the Eucharist?

No, deacons may *never* "preside" at the Eucharist, since deacons are not ordained to the priesthood. In some areas suffering a shortage of priests, it might seem tempting to "authorize" deacons to preside at the Eucharist, but this would be inconsistent with our sacramental understanding of the diaconate, the priesthood, and the Eucharist itself. In the absence of a priest, the deacon may, of course, preside over the community's *worship;* in fact, the deacon is the logical minister to do so. Nonetheless, he may *not* preside at a Eucharist.

77. Do deacons "hear confessions"?

Deacons do not "hear confessions" (the sacrament of penance or reconciliation) or give absolution. The celebrant of the sacrament of reconciliation must always be a priest or bishop.

78. Why don't deacons celebrate the sacrament of the anointing of the sick?

This is a question that many people ask today, especially as more and more deacons are involved in hospital ministry. Here are two points of reflection, one looking solely at the sacrament of anointing itself, and the second based on the context of the anointing.

When thinking about the sacrament of anointing the sick, people sometimes turn to the letter of James:

> Are any among you sick? They should call for the elders of the church and have them pray over them, anointing them with oil in the name of the Lord. The prayer of faith will save the sick, and the Lord will raise them up; and anyone who has committed sins will be forgiven. Therefore confess your sins to one another, and pray for one another, so that you may be healed. The prayer of the righteous is powerful and effective. (James 5:14–16)

This passage is quite interesting because not only does it speak to the way the Christian community ought to act in the face of illness, but it also shows us a pattern to follow. It would be mistaken, however, to read into the text our contemporary understanding of "priests" for the word "elders." (Certainly, the Greek word *presbyteroi* for "elders" would later become the source of the English word *priests*. However, the nature and ministry of the priesthood is impossible to determine with any great detail from the New Testament alone.)

The passage also reveals another interesting dimension that has long been associated with the pastoral care of the sick, and that is the forgiveness of sins. As time passed and pastoral practice evolved, this connection was formalized into what became known as the "last rites" for the dying. When a person speaks, even today, of the last rites, three things are included: the anointing of the sick person, the confession of sins and sacramental absolution, and the reception of viaticum (holy communion given to the dying). Since in pastoral practice all three dimensions of the last rites are desired, and only priests may hear confessions and give sacramental absolution, it is the current law of the Church that only priests may anoint the sick as well. Deacons, however, are ordinary ministers of viaticum.

79. Since deacons don't preside at Mass, does that mean deacons can only witness marriages *outside* of Mass?

Deacons may witness marriages that are celebrated during Mass; it simply means that a priest must also be present to preside at the Mass. There are two sacraments involved here: the celebration of the Eucharist (Mass) and the celebration of matrimony. When the time comes for the celebration of matrimony, the deacon simply comes forward and presides at that ceremony. The same can be said about celebrations of baptisms within the Eucharist. Deacons often preside at baptisms within a Mass presided over by the pastor or another priest.

The situation in the Eastern Catholic Churches is different, however, since these Churches have their own laws concerning the celebration of the sacraments. In the case of matrimony, Eastern law requires, in addition to the exchange of vows between the bride and groom, the formal blessing by the priest. This means that, for a marriage to be valid in the eyes of the Eastern Catholic Church, the priest's blessing is necessary. Therefore, Eastern Catholic deacons, unlike their Latin Rite counterparts, do not witness marriages.

80. Can deacons ordain other deacons?

Only bishops may ordain anyone, because through their own sacramental ordination as bishops they receive the fullness of the apostolic ministry. Priests and deacons do not ordain.

81. A friend of mine said that the deacon in her parish often presides at funerals, and last night I saw a deacon conducting a wake service. Are deacons supposed to do these things?

Deacons are authorized to preside at funerals, wake services, and other gatherings of the assembly at prayer. All of these functions are spelled out in the various liturgical books and in the *Code of Canon Law*.

82. Do deacons lead other kinds of prayer services?

Through ordination deacons share in the responsibility for the prayer life of the community. Deacons may lead various Liturgies of the Word and other services, such as public recitations of the Rosary, Exposition and Benediction of the Blessed Sacrament, Stations of the Cross, and so on. The deacon may also preside at various rites connected with the Rite of Christian Initiation of Adults (RCIA).

83. I've heard that deacons have a responsibility to "pray daily the Liturgy of the Hours." What is this Liturgy of the Hours, and how does it involve deacons?

The Liturgy of the Hours is the public daily prayer of the Church. While the Eucharist is the "source and summit" of our lives as Christians, the Liturgy of the Hours is the *official* daily prayer of the Church. From early in the life of the Church, there was a desire to "sanctify time"—to follow the scriptural command to "pray always and not to lose heart" (Luke 18:1). Eventually monastic communities began praying at specific "hours" throughout the day, and this is the basis for what we now refer to as the Liturgy of the Hours (also known as "Hours" or "The Divine Office"). Heavily scriptural, the prayers are structured around the psalms. Following the liturgical reforms of the Second Vatican Council, the Liturgy of the Hours is composed of Morning Prayer (formerly known as *Lauds*), Daytime Prayer (formerly known as

Terce, Sext, and *None,* and which consists of midmorning, midday, and midafternoon Prayer), Evening Prayer (formerly known as *Vespers*), Night Prayer (formerly known as *Compline*), and Readings (formerly known as *Matins* or *Vigils,* and which have no specific designated time).

Canon law obliges permanent deacons to pray those portions of the Liturgy of the Hours as determined by the Conference of Bishops. In the United States, the United States Conference of Catholic Bishops has directed that permanent deacons are to pray Morning Prayer and Evening Prayer. This constitutes the obligation; however, many deacons pray the entire Liturgy of the Hours for the sake of the Church.

84. Can deacons bless people and things?

A blessing calls upon God to be with a person in a special way, or to set aside something for a sacred purpose. In accordance with the various liturgical books, deacons may give blessings, and this means that deacons can generally bless most religious artifacts, just as priests do. Deacons also bless people, especially in connection with various sacramental rites or liturgical services.

Unfortunately, it's not unusual for a person to come up to the deacon after Mass and ask if Father is available to bless a rosary or similar religious article. The deacon may offer to conduct the blessing, but some people will say, "Oh, I want Father to do it," or "I didn't know deacons could bless things."

85. I have heard that the deacon has special liturgical functions during Holy Week. What is Holy Week, and how does the deacon function during this special time?

Holy Week is the most sacred time of our entire liturgical year. The week begins with Palm (or "Passion") Sunday and extends through Holy Saturday. Holy Thursday, Good Friday, and Holy Saturday are known collectively as the *Triduum* (Latin for "the three days"). These three days are in essence one celebration spread across the period.

Perhaps it is even better to refer to it in musical terms. The Triduum is like a piece of music in three movements; let's take a closer look at several parts that have particular relevance for deacons. The first movement of the Triduum is the celebration of the Lord's Supper on Holy Thursday. This Mass is frequently associated with the establishment of the Eucharist (and the priesthood) by Christ at the Last Supper. It is also during the Mass on Holy Thursday that we find the "washing of feet," which has particular importance for deacons. A careful reading of the Gospel account reveals that there is more involved with this act than simple menial service. Scripture scholars tell us that the washing of the disciples' feet by Christ is a foreshadowing of his own death, and his challenge to his apostles to follow his example is actually a call to follow him into the depth of the paschal mystery. It is in this model of Christ pouring himself out in service that the deacon finds his own sacramental nature.

On Good Friday, the Church commemorates Christ's death and burial. It is the one day of the liturgical year in which we do *not* celebrate the Mass. During the Liturgy of the Word, the deacon rightly proclaims the Gospel (which, in this case, is the passion account). During the extended General Intercessions, the deacon introduces each of the intercessions and directs the assembly to kneel and stand. The deacon may assist with the Veneration of the Cross, and then he brings the reserved hosts, consecrated at the Mass of the Lord's Supper on Holy Thursday, to the altar for the distribution of communion.

The week culminates with the great Easter Vigil after sunset on Holy Saturday. This is truly the heart and soul of the liturgical year, in which the Church herself passes through death to new life. The vigil begins a Service of Light, and the deacon has a crucial part in this service. After the darkness of death experienced on Good Friday, the Church gathers, and the bishop (or local pastor) lights and blesses a new fire. Then the Easter candle (also referred to as the paschal candle) is brought forward and lit. A procession by the faithful into the church is led by the deacon carrying the lit candle. Three times the deacon pauses on the way into the darkened church to proclaim, "Christ, our Light!" The people respond, "Thanks be to God!" Once the candle is placed in its holder in the sanctuary, the deacon chants an ancient hymn known as the Exsultet. This beautiful prayer recounts the great acts of salvation history in which God's covenant people are brought into new life through Christ. It is the deacon who has the honor and the responsibility to bring the light of Christ to the assembly and to sing Christ's praises as the vigil begins.

Following the Service of Light, the vigil continues with an extended Liturgy of the Word. The deacon participates as he does in any Mass, as the ordinary proclaimer of the Gospel. Following the Liturgy of the Word, the vigil continues with the sacraments of initiation, and the deacon assists the bishop or pastor with the baptisms, receptions into full communion, and confirmations. Finally, during the Liturgy of the Eucharist, the deacon exercises his normal functions. At the end of the Mass, it is the deacon who sends the newly reborn community back into the world with the dismissal, now expanded by the great double Alleluia to stress the great joy of Easter.

For all Catholics, Holy Week (and in particular the Triduum) summarizes, symbolizes, and celebrates the most central aspects of our faith. The diaconal identity of the Church is a constitutive element woven through the entire three days, and deacons approach their responsibilities during the Triduum with awe and reverence.

86. What liturgical vestments do deacons wear, and what is their significance?

As members of the clergy, deacons wear during Mass many of the same basic vestments as priests and bishops. This includes the *amice* (a rectangular linen cloth used to cover the wearer's neckwear), if necessary. The *General Instruction of the Roman*

Missal (GIRM) says, "An amice should be put on first if the alb does not completely cover the street clothing at the neck." The *alb* (the name comes from the Latin word for *white*) is a long white robe. Although we usually see only the clergy wearing albs, its true significance lies in the fact that it represents the white garment presented to *all* Christians at baptism. For this reason the GIRM states, "The vestment common to ministers of every rank is the alb...." Finally, if the alb is large, a cincture (a rope-belt) may be worn to adjust the fit of the alb for ease of movement.

Vestments unique to the deacon include the *stole* and the *dalmatic*. Although the stole is worn by all members of the clergy, it is worn in a unique way by the deacon. The stole is a long, narrow piece of cloth worn around the neck of the minister. The Council of Toledo (AD 633) directed that the deacon wear his stole over his left shoulder and caught up at the right hip, because "the right side he must have free, in order that he may without hindrance, do his service."

Stoles are worn over the alb (and cincture) but under the dalmatic. The dalmatic was originally an ordinary garment in the Roman province of Dalmatia. By the fourth century, the dalmatic was worn over the alb by bishops and deacons. By the ninth century, the Western church decreed that, at Mass, the priest wore a chasuble over the alb, and the deacon wore a dalmatic. The dalmatic is the deacon's vestment that parallels the priest's chasuble. It is a knee-length (or longer) vestment made with sleeves and slit down the sides. As a general rule, if a priest wears a chasuble, the deacon should wear a dalmatic. Like the chasuble, it is in the color of the liturgical season. The liturgical colors for these vestments are white for Easter and Christmas seasons (also funeral Masses and Masses associated with the Blessed Virgin Mary), violet during Lent and Advent, red on Palm Sunday, Good Friday, Pentecost, feasts of the Holy Spirit, and feasts of martyrs, green for Ordinary Time, and rose (an optional color) for *Gaudete* Sunday during Advent and *Laetare* Sunday during Lent.

SEVEN

DEACONS AS APOSTOLIC LEADERS IN SERVICE

> The basic spiritual attitude of the deacon... must include a perceptive eye for those suffering distress, illness or fear. The task is to bring a healing that sets them free and empowers them to trust and so to serve and love others.
>
> Cardinal Walter Kasper, *The Diaconate*

87. What does it mean to describe deacons as "apostolic leaders in service"?

This is a term used to summarize the deacon's ministry. As an "apostolic" minister, the deacon has a share in the apostolic ministry of the diocesan bishop. As such, the deacon himself becomes an "apostle": one who is sent to proclaim the risen Christ. The second term can be a little trickier. Some deacons like to say that they are not leaders, they are servants. I think such a statement reveals an inadequate understanding of leadership. *Leadership,* as mentioned above, is not the same as *management;* leadership has a spiritual dimension to it and a focus on people, while management tends to look at resources. Some of our greatest leaders in society and the Church have been terrible managers, and some of our best managers have been terrible leaders! The point is that ordination to any order, including the diaconate, involves a responsibility for leadership. Deacons are to be "servant-leaders," bringing out the spiritual and servant dimensions of leadership to the Church and the world. Christ taught the style of Christian leadership in Mark 10:42 when he contrasts how "the Gentiles" lead with how the Christian should lead, or in John 13 when he washes the feet of the disciples, telling them that they need to go out and pour out their lives for others. This kind of leadership is best exemplified by the third term: *service.* Deacons are particular leaders in demonstrating and witnessing the profound self-sacrifice that Christians should make in service to others. This is at least some of what is meant by the expression "apostolic leaders in service."

88. What did Pope Paul VI mean when he referred to deacons as a "driving force of the Church's service"?

The English expression "driving force" is the usual translation of the Latin word *animator*. It's interesting to see this original word, given its similarity to the word *anima* or *soul*. I believe that what the pope was referring to is the responsibility of deacons to be the soul of the Church's own identity of *diakonia*. There is also a very dynamic image here: an animator is someone who brings life to something, and the deacon ought to be bringing life to the Church's service to others. He should be a minister that inspires, inflames, and empowers others to their own diaconal responsibilities.

89. If deacons are "servants," how can they be leaders?

As in question 87, our understanding of leadership is distinct from that of management. A leader is a person who is capable of articulating a vision for others and then inspiring and empowering others to move toward making that vision a reality. In most cases and in many different groups, leadership is a function exercised by any number of people within a group, and not always by the one who has an official title or position of overall leadership. For example, we can all identify circumstances when an executive's assistant actually exercises more leadership in certain aspects than the executive. Just try to see a doctor or a lawyer or any other professional without first working with their assistant or secretary!

Leadership is also exercised in less formal, but no less influential ways. Nonetheless, ordination to any order—bishop, deacon, or priest—involves the assumption of leadership responsibilities for the good of the community. For deacons, this means a unique responsibility for servant-leadership.[45]

90. Are deacons supposed to do more about charity and justice than simply serve in a variety of charitable works?

Because deacons should be leaders in service, they should be dedicated not only to doing certain charitable works, but also to attempting to deal with the underlying social, economic, and political roots of the problems affecting those who are most in need. This means that deacons must often become engaged with the very structures of society in an attempt to transform those structures through the work of the laity. The deacon should also inspire the laity to take a more active role in societal transformation, through his official teaching and preaching. It ought to be the deacon who helps the entire Church realize the connection between the worship and love of God and the care and protection of others.

91. Aren't *all* Christians supposed to serve the needs of others?

Absolutely. It is the role of the laity to transform society at large. The role of the deacon is often to challenge the *entire* community in concrete, pastoral terms to live out this responsibility. The role of the deacon is not to usurp the role of the laity, but to help assure the laity of the presence of Christ and the support of the whole Church in their own unique role to be the "soul and leaven" of society. The deacon's role is one of servant-leadership.

92. How do deacons exercise this ministry?

Deacons can exercise this ministry of justice and peace in a variety of ways. They most often do so through their own direct involvement in social justice issues in the community. They also preach and teach and provide leadership to parish and diocesan groups dedicated to these ministries.

93. *Where* do deacons exercise this ministry?

Cardinal Walter Kasper has written that "the deacon's place is in these marginal areas of church and society, where breakthroughs can occur."[46] He then provides a remarkable list of places and activities for diaconal ministry. I have avoided long quotes in this text, but Cardinal Kasper's suggestions are so practical and insightful, they deserve to be highlighted:

> The deacon can and must become the public advocate of the weak and powerless and of all those who have no other voice or lobby....One essential task consists in finding, training, and guiding volunteer church workers....Ideally, the deacon should initiate and support self-help groups, e.g., for single parents or drug addicts.[47]

While the deacon is probably assigned to a particular parish, that particular parish, says Kasper, can serve as a kind of nerve-center for wider diaconal activity:

> His ministry should have a wider scope [e.g., for a city, a deanery, or a region]. With his base in one parish, he could build up the diaconal tasks in several communities and link these in a network....As the official representative of the community, he is the obvious contact person for regional Catholic charity organizations and health centers....He should also ensure that the communities are in contact with those responsible for social matters in local government and in nongovernmental aid organizations....The deacons of a diocese also form an advisory body that can be very helpful to the bishop; as a fellowship, they can be the bishop's eyes and ears with respect to human needs, and they can help him to be the "father of the poor."[48]

94. Are deacons parish ministers or diocesan ministers?

Ordination to ministry is always centered around the needs of a particular diocese, not simply the needs of a given parish. In the early days of the diaconate, deacons were often nominated for formation by their pastors, who did so expecting that the deacon would remain in his home parish and help out. This was most often the case.

Today, however, the Church has realized that deacons are *not* ordained simply for one's home parish. Through sacramental ordination, a deacon takes on a responsibility for the pastoral care of the entire diocese, under the leadership of the diocesan bishop. While many deacons continue to serve in their original parishes, they are increasingly being given new assignments as the needs of the diocese become more clear. Certainly a deacon, especially one who is married or employed in a particular area, cannot be moved indiscriminately. In such cases, considerable discussion is held between all parties involved, including the deacon's wife. In more urban areas, of course, it is much easier to ask a deacon to assume responsibilities at a neighboring parish. In more rural areas, however, this might not be possible. In other cases, deacons are at a time in their lives when they are ready to relocate, and the ecclesiastical assignment coincides with that relocation. The key here, though, is that the deacon, through his ordination, takes on a share of the bishop's responsibility for the entire diocese.

95. If a deacon grew up in one parish, why would the bishop send him to another parish?

The simplest answer is often the best: upon ordination the deacon may be assigned wherever the bishop feels the needs are greatest and where the particular deacon's skills and gifts can be put to optimum use. In some cases, deacons have been in the same parish so long that they are perceived (and may even perceive themselves) to be "the parish's deacon" rather than the diocese's deacon.

96. Can a parish have more than one deacon?

One of the more pleasant problems some areas are facing with the dramatic *increase* of deacons in many parts of the country is where they are to be assigned. Some parishes have seven, eight, or even more deacons! This can be a blessing, but there is also a cautionary note. With the resurgence of the diaconate, the distribution of deacons has become an issue in some parts of the country; one parish may have multiple deacons, but the other parishes in town have none. Bishops are now ensuring that the distribution of deacons (as well as priests) is more equitable and able to meet the needs of parishioners.

97. Can a deacon serve in more than one parish?

Just as we have priests serving more than one parish at a time, there are deacons doing the same thing. As you've probably seen by now in many of these answers, the deacon is a diocesan minister at the disposal of the bishop. If there is a need anywhere in the diocese, the bishop may ask one or more of his deacons to try to address it.

98. Our deacon serves as a chaplain at the county jail. Do all deacons serve in assignments outside a parish, and can they be called "chaplains"?

Since deacons are ministers of the entire diocesan church, the bishop makes the ultimate determination where the deacon's particular gifts and talents may best be put to use. Deacons should serve wherever the need is greatest, and often times that is outside the parish. There are great needs within the parish itself that demand the deacon's attention, but there are additional needs outside the parish, and the deacon has a responsibility to help meet those needs.

In some dioceses, deacons receive a two-part assignment: The first part of the assignment is to a local parish for the deacon's exercise of the ministry of Word and Sacrament; often the second part of the assignment is to some regional or diocesan institution (such as a hospital or prison) for the exercise of the deacon's ministry of Charity. Just as a priest shares with the bishop the responsibility for pastoral life beyond the parish in which he's serving, so, too, the deacon has a similar wide-ranging responsibility.

The term "chaplain" requires some explanation. Some people interpret canon law as saying that only priests can have the title "chaplain." Others interpret it a bit more broadly and suggest that others might also legitimately hold that title. Adding to the confusion, of course, is the fact that many times the institutions themselves, even those that are not Catholic, use the term "chaplain" in an even more general way. We will not be able to resolve this debate here. For our purposes we can simply say that deacons assist in many ways, full-time and part-time, in prisons, hospitals, and nursing homes.

99. What diocesan offices are open to deacons?

It's probably easier to list the diocesan offices that are reserved to priests (and therefore are not open to deacons) than to list all of the possibilities for deacons. Under current canon law, only a priest may serve as a "vicar" of the bishop; this means that a deacon may not serve as the vicar general of a diocese; similarly he may not serve as the judicial vicar of a diocese, or as an episcopal vicar, such as the dean of a deanery. Looked at more positively, then, deacons may serve (assuming they have the requisite academic background and experience) as chief financial officer, as the department head of a group of offices at the diocese, as a judge on the diocesan tribunal, as the superintendent of Catholic schools for a diocese, and so on. With the exception of those few offices reserved to priests, deacons may serve in almost any capacity, as suggested by his qualifications and the needs of the diocese.

100. Do deacons serve in national and international roles of service?

Deacons are serving in an astonishing variety of roles around the world. In addition to ministries within the Church at diocesan, regional, and national levels, many deacons are providing servant-leadership through their secular professions and interests. Some deacons are involved in international programs of humanitarian and missionary outreach; others serve on boards of charitable institutions. What is important is that deacons everywhere make full use of their unique God-given gifts and talents, just as all Christians are called to do. But in the case of the deacon, there is the added dimension of being a member of the clergy; his activities often reflect the official and institutional concern of the entire Church for particular needs and concerns.

FINAL REFLECTION

The ecclesiology of *communio* makes the ministry of the permanent deacon a necessity. He represents Jesus Christ, the good shepherd who goes in search of the strayed sheep and is willing to lay down his own life in the attempt.

Cardinal Walter Kasper, *The Diaconate*

101. A parishioner recently said she hoped that all the problems of the Church would soon be solved, and there would no longer be any need for the permanent diaconate since there would be enough priests and lay persons to handle everything. When will we know we have enough deacons?

Although the diaconate has been around from the very beginning of the Church, in terms of the restored and renewed permanent diaconate, however, it is still a new reality, and we are all still learning about the potential of the diaconate. It is natural that for these first decades there has been a focus on the functions deacons may or may not perform. However, as time goes by, it is becoming increasingly apparent that the real significance of the diaconate is less about their functions than their essence as *sacramental signs* of Christ himself. The implications of this reality need considerable development. Bishops and pastors need to remember that deacons are not ordained simply to supply functions that might be in short supply because of shortage of priests; deacons need to be reminded that they must always dig deeper into the radical nature of their responsibilities. Through ordination, deacons are to be servant-leaders who meet the needs of others through direct service and through inspirational and prophetic leadership. This leadership, while always exercised under the authority of the diocesan bishop, is conferred by the Holy Spirit on the deacon through his sacramental ordination. It is in response to the example of Christ and the power of the Spirit that the deacon exercises his ministry of witness, worship, and charity.

In response to this question, then, we can say that there will *always* be a need for more deacons. Even if the Church were graced with thousands of priestly ordinations tomorrow, there would still be a need for deacons, just as there will always be a need for lay persons to exercise their own unique ministries in the

Church and the world. Over time, we had lost this sense of diaconal and lay ministries; the Second Vatican Council opened the
windows and encouraged the Church to rediscover them.

On June 17, 2001, the Rev. Irma Wyman, Archdeacon for
the Diaconate for the Episcopal Diocese of Minnesota, delivered
a sermon entitled "Holy Rescuers," in which she asked, "How
will we know when we have enough deacons?" Her answer—

> When all the needs of the marginalized and vulnerable are
> met.
>
> When to gather the gifts of the church and take them
> to the world, and to gather needs of the world and bring
> them to the church, has become a habit.
>
> When…"deacons, going back and forth, have worn
> down the boundary lines that we use to keep church and
> world separated."
>
> When deacons, leading the baptized in and out, have
> beaten a path between the altar and the gutter so that every-
> one will see the link between the Blood in our chalices and
> the blood in our streets.
>
> When all people respond to the challenge to live, not
> in the love of power but in the power of love.[49]

Deacons—and the Deacon-Church in which they serve—
have their challenges clearly stated. Consider the famous passage
of Matthew 25:31–46. The day of judgment is described in terms
of how well we respond to the needs of others. Sitting on the
throne of judgment, Christ, surrounded by angels, selects those to
be saved:

> For I was hungry and you gave me food, I was thirsty and
> you gave me something to drink. I was a stranger and you
> welcomed me, I was naked and you gave me clothing, I was
> sick and you took care of me, I was in prison and you vis-
> ited me.

Conversely, those who do not do these things are damned.

All of us privileged and challenged to call ourselves Christ's disciples are going to be judged in these terms. Those who serve the rest as deacons bear a unique responsibility, not only to fulfill their own diaconal obligations as disciples, but to pour themselves out in servant-leadership for others. They are not simply to perform acts of diaconal service, as important as they are; they are to lead, inspire, and support the rest of the Church in living out the full demands of discipleship.

The work of Carol Gilligan provides a wonderful coda to our reflection on the integration of the diaconate into the ministerial life of the Church. In her now-classic text *In a Different Voice,* Gilligan found that earlier attempts to describe human moral development had been flawed by an exclusive dependence upon male subjects.[50] The results of that prior research had created a matrix of moral development that, when applied to girls or women, seemed to indicate moral development that was less predictable and perhaps even less developed than that of boys and men. Gilligan discovered in her own research that girls and women have their own "voice" and their own matrix of moral development. She further suggests that there may be additional voices waiting to be heard, based perhaps on economics or other factors.

Transferring this insight to the diaconate, one may say that the diaconate offers a "different voice" in the contemporary Church. One of the significant contributions of the renewal of the diaconate as a permanent order within the ordained ministries at the service of the people of God is the realization that ordained ministry is not exclusively "priestly" and that the diaconate, in fact, adds a unique dimension of servant-leadership to official ministry. It is, in fact, a "different voice" in the chorus of ordained ministry.

NOTES

1. Paul VI, *motu proprio Sacrum Diaconatus Ordinem,* June 18, 1967: *AAS* 59 (1967), 697–704.

2. Paul VI, *Hodie concilium, AAS* 58 (1966), 57–64.

3. Paul VI, Apostolic Letter *Ad Pascendum* (August 15, 1972), citing Matt 20:28.

4. Richard R. Gaillardetz, "Are Deacons the Answer?" in *Commonweal* CXXX/14 (August 15, 2003): 22–24.

5. *Traditio Apostolica,* 1, 9; trans. B. S. Easton, *The Apostolic Tradition of Hippolytus* (New York: Macmillan, 1934), 38–39.

6. R. Hugh Connolly, *Didascalia Apostolorum: The Syriac Version* (Oxford: Clarendon Press, 1929), 109, 148.

7. Ignatius, *Trallians* 3:1, in *Early Christian Fathers,* ed. Cyril C. Richardson (New York: Collier Books, Macmillan Publishing Co., 1970), 99. Ignatius, *Magnesians* 6:1, in Richardson, 95.

8. Joseph W. Pokusa, "The Archdeacon's Office and Functions in the Decretals of Gregory IX." JCL thesis. Catholic University of America, 1977.

9. Josef Hornef, "The Genesis and Growth of the Proposal," in *Foundations for the Renewal of the Diaconate* (Washington, DC: United States Catholic Conference, 1993), 6; Margret Morche, *Zur Erneuerung des Ständigen Diakonats* (Freiburg: Lambertus-Verlag, 1996), esp. 15–21.

10. Otto Pies, "Block 26: Erfahrungen aus dem Priesterleben in Dachau," *Stimmen der Zeit* 141 (1947–1948): 10–28. Wilhelm Schamoni, *Familienväter als geweihte Diakone* (Paderborn: Schöningh, 1953). English translation: *Married Men as Ordained Deacons,* trans. Otto Eisner (London: Burns and Oates, 1955).

11. Pius XII, "Quelques aspects fondamentaux de l'apostolat des laïcs : Hiérarchie et Apostolat," *AAS* 49 (1957): 925.

12. The documents of the Second Vatican Council are known officially by the first two or three words of the original Latin text, and I will provide those names following the English translation.

13. National Conference of Catholic Bishops, *Permanent Deacons in the United States: Guidelines for Their Formation and Ministry, 1984 Revision* (Washington, DC: NCCB, 1984), #43. Hereafter referred to as *1984 Guidelines*.

14. *Gaudium et Spes* 40.

15. *Lumen Gentium* 21, 22.

16. Ibid., 22.

17. Ibid., 26, 27.

18. *The Roman Pontifical as Renewed by Decree of the Second Vatican Council, Published by Authority of Pope Paul VI and Further Revised at the Direction of Pope John Paul II. Rites of Ordination of a Bishop, of Priests, and of Deacons, Second Typical Edition* (Washington, DC: United States Conference of Catholic Bishops, 2003), vii.

19. See, for example, John D. Zizioulas, *Being as Communion: Studies in Personhood and the Church* (Crestwood, NY: St. Vladimir's Seminary Press, 1985), 216.

20. John Paul II, catechesis at the General Audience of October 6, 1993, *Deacons Serve the Kingdom of God, #6, in Insegnamenti* XVI, 2 (1993), 954.

21. Canon 1031, §2. All references to canon law in the Latin Rite are from the Canon Law Society of America, *New Commentary on the Code of Canon Law: An Entirely New and Comprehensive Commentary by Canonists from North America and Europe, with a Revised English Translation of the Code* (Mahwah, NJ: Paulist Press, 2000).

22. Center for Applied Research in the Apostolate, "Profile of the Diaconate in the United States: A Report of Findings from CARA's Deacon Poll" (Washington, DC: CARA, April 2004), 9.

23. John Paul II, post-synodal apostolic exhortation *Pastores Dabo Vobis* (Boston: St. Paul Books and Media, 1992).

24. See, for example, Mark 1:29–31, Matt 8:14–15, and Luke 4:38–39.

25. St. Augustine, *Sermo* 340, 1: *PL* 38, 1483.

26. For a more complete treatment of these data, see Richard A. Schoenherr and L. A. Young, *Full Pews & Empty Altars: Demographics of the Priest Shortage in United States Catholic Dioceses* (Madison, WI: University of Wisconsin Press, 1993), 171–73.

27. John Paul II, *Ordinatio Sacerdotalis.*

28. See, for example, Phyllis Zagano, *Holy Saturday: An Argument for the Restoration of the Female Diaconate in the Catholic Church* (New York: Crossroad, 2000).

29. 1984 *Guidelines,* #130.

30. 1984 *Guidelines,* #131.

31. John Paul II, post-synodal apostolic exhortation *Pastores Gregis* (Vatican City: Libreria Editrice Vaticana, 2003), #49.

32. Jordan Hite, TOR, and Daniel J. Ward, OSB, *Readings, Cases, Materials in Canon Law: A Textbook for Ministerial Students,* revised edition (Collegeville, MN: The Liturgical Press, 1990), 472.

33. Walter Kasper, "The Diaconate," in *Leadership in the Church: How Traditional Roles Can Serve the Christian Community Today* (New York: Crossroad, 2003), 18. Originally published as "Der Diakon in ekklesiologisher Sicht angesichts der gegenwärtigen Herausforderungen in Kirche und Gesellschaft," in *Diakonia* 32/3–4 (1997), 13–33; also in W. Kasper, *Theologie und Kirche* (Mainz: Matthias-Grünewald, 1999), 2:145–62; and as "The Ministry of the Deacon: The Deacon Offers an Ecclesiological View of Current Challenges in the Church and Society," *Deacon Digest* (March/April 1998), 20.

34. Kasper, "The Diaconate," 18.

35. Center for Applied Research in the Apostolate. "The Permanent Diaconate Today: A Research Report by the Bishops' Committee on the Diaconate of the NCCB and by the Center for Applied Research in the Apostolate" (Washington, DC: CARA, June 2000).

36. John Paul II, "Apostles of the New Evangelization," Address to Permanent Deacons and their Families During the Jubilee Day for Deacons, February 19, 2000, in *L'Osservatore Romano,* English Language Edition, February 23, 2000, 3.

37. *Roman Pontifical.*

38. Canon 764.

39. Congregation for Catholic Education, *Basic Norms for the Formation of Permanent Deacons* (Washington, DC: United States Catholic Conference, 1998), #9.

40. *Lumen Gentium,* #11.

41. Ibid.

42. *Sacrosanctum Concilium,* #2.

43. Ibid., #10.

44. Ibid., #14.

45. Robert K. Greenleaf, *Servant Leadership: A Journey into the Nature of Legitimate Power and Greatness* (New York: Paulist Press, 1977).

46. Kasper, "The Diaconate," 36.

47. Ibid., 41.

48. Ibid., 41–43.

49. Irma M. Wyman, "Holy Rescuers," in *Soundings* 23:4 (August 2001), 11.

50. Carol Gilligan, *In a Different Voice* (Cambridge, MA: Harvard University Press, 1983).

RESPONSES TO 101 QUESTIONS ON THE PSALMS
AND OTHER WRITINGS
by Roland E. Murphy, O. Carm.

RESPONSES TO 101 QUESTIONS ON DEATH AND
ETERNAL LIFE
by Peter C. Phan

RESPONSES TO 101 QUESTIONS ON HINDUISM
by John Renard

RESPONSES TO 101 QUESTIONS ON BUDDHISM
by John Renard

RESPONSES TO 101 QUESTIONS ON THE MASS
by Kevin W. Irwin

RESPONSES TO 101 QUESTIONS ON GOD AND EVOLUTION
by John F. Haught

RESPONSES TO 101 QUESTIONS ON
CATHOLIC SOCIAL TEACHING
by Kenneth R. Himes, O.F.M.